Advantage Contractor

Business Success Series

Volume 3:

Project Scheduling for Construction Contractors

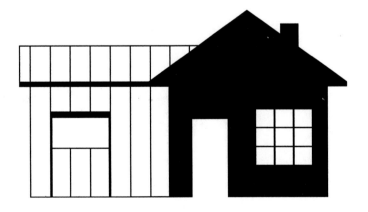

Gene Fessenbecker

About the Construction Contracting Academy

The Academy was founded in 1991 by Gene Fessenbecker to provide materials any independent contractor could use to start a contracting business correctly or to improve one that was operating. Shortly thereafter, the Oregon Legislature adopted a law requiring new contractors in Oregon to take 16 hours of education in "Laws and Business Practices Affecting Contractors." Gene took his information and set up the first written home study courses on the business of construction contracting. These courses were accredited by the Oregon Construction Contractors Board and still set the standard by which this type of course is judged.

Now these courses and others are available to all those people who want to do their trade as a business, as well as those who want to set up a contracting firm and hire trades people. The courses offered by the Academy through this Series allow you to start and operate a contracting business with more comfort by reducing the risk you face. Through the study of these courses and implementation of the routines and practices you can rise above the average and achieve business success in construction contracting.

Publisher's Cataloging-in-Publication
(Provided by Quality Books, Inc.)

Fessenbecker, Gene.
    Advantage Contractor Business Success Series / Gene
Fessenbecker. -- 1st ed.
        v. cm.
    Includes bibliographical references and index.
    Preassigned LCCN: 97-078290
    ISBN: 1-888198-17-6

    1. Construction industry--Management--United States.
I. Title. II. Title: Advantage Contractor Business Success
Series

HD9715.U6F47 1998   338.4769'068
                                QBI98-451

Published by **Construction Contracting Press**,
a division of the **Construction Contracting Academy**
83 Centennial Loop • Eugene, Oregon 97401 • (541) 344-1442 •
1-800-937-2242 • (541) 344-5387 Fax   www.acbss.com

Advantage Contractor Business Success Series

About the Author

Gene Fessenbecker, author and President of the Construction Contracting Academy, has done remodeling, custom home building, restoration and repairs as a general contractor, and worked as manager and operator of four different construction businesses over a period of 20 years. Gene wrote thirteen accredited self-study courses for the Oregon Contractors Prerequisite Education Program which have been offered through the Construction Contracting Academy since 1992. Currently, in addition to writing about the business of construction contracting, he is a dispute settler for home owner and home inspection warranty programs. Gene lives in Eugene, OR in a house that he has remodeled twice in the last 16 years.

Doing Your Part in Using this Book

We have done our best to provide useful and accurate information in this book. Every precaution has been taken to give you a product that you can use to build a productive contracting business. You have to take the information and use it as presented and do the work of operating a business, as described, to gain the best results. However, neither the publisher nor the author assumes any liability for damages incurred through the use of this book.

Special Thanks

The Advantage Contractor Business Success Series is a product of many special people. At the beginning of the Oregon Contractor Education Program Joe DeMarzo was instrumental in getting courses into finished condition. Laura Stine took many organizational and personnel challenges and found solutions. Don Sirkin provided financing to the fledgling company. Linda Seaman and Liz Overstreet made many changes to stabilize the growing business. Later all of these efforts are brought to bear on this Series. Angela Lewis and Linda Seaman made the difference as the new courses grew into being. Thanks to these and all the others who had a hand in the success of the Academy.

Contents

Chapter 3: Scheduling Systems

Table of Exhibits and Figures

About This Series

"There is only one success-to be able to spend life in your own way."
Christopher Morley

For most people who go into it, construction contracting is a way of practicing a construction trade. For others it can be a means of doing business. The *Advantage Contractor Business Success Series* is designed mainly for tradespeople who are running a contracting business. However, even seasoned business people can benefit from the information in this course.

Contractor business records from around the country show that fewer than one in five firms survive the first five years of business. Nationwide an average of 20 percent of new contractors are not in business at the end of the first year.

Going into any business is risky. Most businesses that fail do not return the initial amount invested. One of the main benefits in starting a contracting business seems to be the low start-up costs. Perhaps the ease of getting started, and the lower apparent risk, brings people into contracting who are not prepared to stay in business. The *Advantage Contractor Business Success Series* came about to fill this lack of business skill among contractors.

Rules of Business

Many individuals do succeed in the contracting business. The Academy believes successful contractors have learned the rules of business and follow them every day.

The rules of business exist to serve us. Often business rules have to be adapted carefully to a specific business to be of the most use. Therefore, the goal of this series of courses is to put these rules in your hands, like your trade tools, so you can use them effectively.

All I ask is an honest advantage.

Rules of Business as Tools of Business

All tools have to be ready to use and in good condition to be useful, whether they are for trade or for business. In addition, one has to know how to use the tools well. Knowing where the tools are is only part of the solution. Using any tool skillfully takes instruction and practice.

Most of you have worked hard to learn your trade. Now you can enjoy applying the skills of your trade and take pride in your work.

The skills of operating a business are strange and different for most new contractors. It takes time and effort to learn your business skills as well as you have learned your trade. However, as a contractor, you need these business skills as much as your trade skills.

The Academy has combined information from a number of business professionals with the knowledge of contracting. We know first hand what construction contracting is about.

Money Making Tools for Your Business Workbelt^{SM}

The information acquired from the *Advantage Contractor Business Success Series* allows you to keep improving your business skills.

New information has to be worked into your routines to be useful. You will have to make room for the new, more useful information while you discard the old. This is similar to taking an old, worn out tool from your workbelt and replacing it with a new, more useful tool.

To keep improving your contracting business, you will want to keep the most useful and up-to-date tools in your business workbelt. To do this, you can take advantage of the 30 years of contracting and business experience I bring to this course. The successful use of business tools is critical to a new contractor. I can help you with your business right away by giving you specific information you can put to use today.

Self-Paced Personal Instruction

One of the easiest ways to learn as a part-time student is through a home-study course. You study when you have some extra time and where you can be most comfortable.

For an adult, self-paced personal instruction usually offers the most useful educational experience. You can set your own pace, your own time to study, and the amount of effort you want to put into the material. In this way you receive the greatest personal benefit for the time you spend.

"I am convinced that it is of primordial importance to learn more every year than the year before. After all, what is education but a process by which a person begins to learn how to learn."
Peter Ustinov

"Success is merely a matter of luck. Ask any failure."
Earl Wilson

About This Course

A building site can look like pure chaos. The building that comes from this activity is the result of the person doing the project scheduling, the guiding hand.

The Construction Contracting Academy welcomes the opportunity to provide you with the *Advantage Contractor Business Success Series* course, *Project Scheduling for Construction Contractors*.

Project scheduling is a business tool any general contractor has to use in order to keep contractual promises of completion, as well as estimates of labor, in line.

Purpose

This course provides the information you can use to keep your construction projects under control. You will learn "good" scheduling practices and why scheduling is important.

After finishing this course, you should be able to set up a schedule that enables you to track multiple projects and meet your deadlines. Good scheduling is good organization.

Benefits

A general contractor often works on more than one project at a time. All projects may not actually be in the construction stage; you will have sales, bidding, construction, and call-back work (often occurring at the same time).

Organizing your projects with good scheduling techniques helps you manage the internal activities of your construction business. Through effective scheduling, you can smooth out cycles in your business and maintain the balance between over-commitment and idle time.

"Never confuse motion with action."
Ernest Hemingway

Organization

There are three chapters in this course. These chapters will teach you how to:

- Complete your projects promptly
- Keep projects within budget
- Maintain high quality on each project

- Maximize your profit from each project.

Chapter 1: General Scheduling

This chapter covers:

- Time and production management
- Organizational skills used to coordinate construction and maintain control of your project
- A sample residential project schedule outline

*"I think knowing what you **cannot** do is more important than knowing what you **can** do."*
Lucille Ball

Chapter 2: Dealing with Others on the Project

This chapter covers:

- Communicating with all people working on a project
- Using scheduling for total project efficiency

Chapter 3: Scheduling Systems

This chapter covers methods of estimating project time and three different scheduling systems, including:

- The critical path method
- Bar chart scheduling
- Calendar scheduling

Quick Reference Tool

The "Quick Reference Tool" at the end of the manual can be compared to a glossary because it defines and explains words and terms mentioned in the text.

You, Our Customer

As our customer, we are happy to demonstrate our customer service to you. As with all our courses, we at the Academy offer our services to you through these courses. If you have questions or problems, we would be happy to talk to you.

State Offices that Provide Small Business Help

You will find a list of states that have services to assist small businesses.

Resources

This section gives you extra sources of information to learn advanced skills and gain extra advantages. Be sure to put the basics of this course into practice before going on to more complex items.

Bibliography

As a contractor you will always have an advantage if you keep studying and learning how to improve the operation of your business. These books can make a difference.

Web Sites

This section of the course will show you where to go on the net for the information you need.

Index

Chapter 1

General Scheduling

Project scheduling enables you to manage the time and the flow of production. With a well organized project schedule you can manage the internal activities of a construction project as well as transition periods between projects.

A project has a definite life span described by the contract. Many different temporary activities go on during this life span.

Proper scheduling keeps life sane for the general contractor and the specialty contractor. It is the best way to keep both personal life and business activities manageable. A chaotic business life negatively affects your personal life.

Scheduling is a balancing act that allows you to attain enough contracts to ensure year round work and still avoid having too much to do.

Over-commitment

Over-commitment can be more damaging to your business's well-being than not having enough work. During slow times, both income and expenses go down. When projects pile up, you may have to break commitments because of scheduling conflicts. That is when your business loses money, just as expenses are peaking.

The danger of a cash shortage is greatest during times of overextension and maximum expense. A cash shortage occurs when the business fails to have the necessary finances to pay bills.

Business Image

The quality of your scheduling affects every aspect of your business's image. Customers, suppliers, and subcontractors can tell how you run your business by the manner in which you maintain the flow of work. Each one wants to know that you can and will do what you say you will do. There is nothing better than a good reputation.

Customer's Perspective

A contractor who has poor scheduling habits rarely has satisfied customers.

A contractor who cannot begin a project on time creates a bad impression that can taint the entire project. Not finishing a project on time because of poor scheduling, which caused delays, is even worse.

Most contractors depend on word-of-mouth advertising along with references from satisfied customers. Bad scheduling is an easy way to destroy a good reputation.

The journey of ten thousand miles begins with one phone call.

Supplier's Perspective

Suppliers want to deliver their materials when you originally call for them. Suppliers often cannot keep items because of lack of storage; they also expect payment on time. If the job has slowed down and payments under the contract terms are delayed to you, the suppliers will still want their money.

Subcontractor's Perspective

Subcontractors will not remain loyal to a general contractor who cannot properly coordinate a project. The general contractor needs to ensure that the project is at the right stage for each of the subcontractors to begin work on time.

It is also the general contractor's responsibility to ensure that subcontractors do not interfere with each other, or interfere with each other's work, while finishing their own part of the project.

Master Coordinator

Scheduling is a coordinating process. The general contractor has to learn to be a master coordinator who effectively blends the schedules of owners, subcontractors, architects, suppliers, bankers, and building inspectors.

While one eye is on the people involved in the contractor's business, the other eye has to focus on the materials needed to finish the project. Special orders have to be arranged well in advance. Timely delivery of materials often dictates the progress of a project.

Coordination Through Organization

Scheduling is a process of organizing production and developing a system for measuring the success of the production process.

A good coordinator is a contractor with an organized scheduling system. An organized scheduling system evolves from an organized business. If your business is constantly run by the "seat of your pants," it is only a matter of time before chaos (bad scheduling) catches up with you.

An organized contractor develops the framework to produce and maintain an efficient scheduling system for every project.

Beginning with the original estimate and continuing through an organized record keeping system, a contractor has to have the basic means necessary to schedule a construction project.

Most trades people do a good job of managing their time while working. However, managing your time and getting others to follow a schedule is a very different situation. As a contractor, you have to look much further ahead and take many more factors into account.

Project Scheduling

Project scheduling includes more than just having the necessary labor, materials, and subcontractors lined up and on the correct project at the right time.

A good project plan will include alternative strategies for parts that are difficult or "time critical."

The construction project schedule involves:

- Prompt project completion
- Quality control
- Budget control

Prompt Completion

Good scheduling makes prompt completion more likely and reduces idle or wasted time. The benefits to the general contractor are:

- Keeping your scheduled projects on time
- Keeping your customer happy (the customer could be the owner, the lender or a prospective owner)
- Getting the most out of a building season in terms of volume and profit

Quality Control

Good scheduling can improve project quality by keeping work flowing. When poor scheduling causes abrupt stops and starts for employees and subcontractors, project quality suffers. This means:

- Less time for workers to pay attention to detail
- More emphasis on speed
- Greater possibilities for mistakes

Budget Control

You don't want $2.00 parts stopping a $70,000 project.

Time equals money. This is a fundamental rule in the construction business. If the project is delayed due to inferior scheduling, it costs you more money to bring the project back on track.

Besides paying overtime to employees and subcontractors, many other factors can increase costs when a project is delayed:

- The cost of supplies and materials can rise.
- If you have ordered the materials but have not completed the project, bills for materials can become due before you can justify billing the owner. Suppliers charge interest on overdue payments.
- Subcontractors cannot wait for you. They may be forced to move on to other projects. The cost of the project increases if you have to use a higher priced subcontractor to replace the one who has moved on.

Setting a Realistic Schedule

The first step in developing a project schedule is realism. A realistic schedule is one that is workable and sequential.

A workable schedule is based on a realistic workday, and the actual number of workers involved with the project. Scheduled operations cannot exceed the ability of your workers to accomplish the work.

A sequential schedule is based on the logical order of building or installation work that a particular construction project should follow.

Note

For your convenience, we have inserted at the end of this chapter, a "Residential Construction Outline" of the sequence of events for a typical residential construction project.

These concepts are basic to any scheduling system. Although these rules may seem obvious, many schedules collapse because of unrealistic work schedules that cause some activity to be scheduled out of sequence.

A schedule made within basic parameters will be more functional. This is a good workable starting point for your own scheduling.

Not matter what your trade or how many trades you know, your work speed and quality level of performance is not the same as a trades person you may hire. In all cases you have to predict how they will perform. You have to use their performance levels in your schedule.

Scheduling Basics

There are many formal scheduling systems. An overview of these methods is in Chapter 2: "Dealing with Others on the Project." Regardless of what system or method you use, the initial steps are always the same:

- Break the project down into phases
- Determine how long each phase will take
- Determine the proper construction sequence of these phases

This is the foundation from which even the most elaborate systems are developed. The process becomes more elaborate as the size and complexity of the project increases.

Basic Tools

You can't keep trouble from coming, but you needn't give it a chair to sit in.

You already have various tools available for building a schedule. Many projects already have the following:

- Estimating sheet (see Exhibit 1, p. 19)
- Project specifications document (Exhibit 2, p. 20)
- Proposal and agreement (see Exhibit 3, pp. 21- 23)

These are good indicators for what many of the tasks on your project will involve.

Begin With the Estimating Sheet

The estimating sheet is where the initial task breakdown occurs. It breaks the project into specific phases and items for estimating the direct costs of a project.

Direct costs are related to those materials, labor and subcontract work used on a construction project. Indirect costs include overhead expenses, business profit, and the time a contractor spends coordinating work activities.

> ### Note
> The *Advantage Contractor Business Success Series* course, *Cash and Finance in Construction Contracting*, focuses on pricing systems that separate "direct costs" from "indirect costs."

A project can move quickly, sometimes very quickly. This is not the case for all projects, however.

Your scheduling process for a particular project begins with the categories already identified on the estimating sheet.

Your estimate sheet is especially useful if you have designed it so that the *cost* categories are listed in the logical construction sequence. For example:

- Permit process
- Site survey
- Excavation
- Foundation
- Framing; etc.

Cost vs. Time

Your estimating sheet may not contain enough detail to schedule everything. Some parts may involve certain processes or details that are not listed on a cost estimate.

An example of this is the curing time needed for a concrete foundation before forms can be removed. These activities are easy to overlook when developing a schedule because they are not in the cost estimate.

Scheduling involves a different focus than cost estimating. When figuring the cost of a project, waiting periods are not as crucial as they are with the scheduling process. A prime example of this is waiting for permits. The waiting period for a permit can be from

A schedule done on time will usually be on budget. You get the benefit of both when the project stays on schedule.

three weeks to three months or longer. However, the monetary cost may be nothing.

The Construction Contract

Include your construction contract as one of your resources for developing a project schedule. The construction contract will outline important criteria that your project schedule has to meet. Some of these criteria are:

- Start and completion dates for each major project task
- Clauses requiring special protection of the owners' property
- Conditions governing debris removal
- Clauses that will spell out any liquidated damages assessed if the project is not completed on time

Note
"Liquidated damage" is money that the owner may be entitled to if a project takes longer than promised in the contract.

Plans and Specs

Combine the initial project breakdown list from your estimating sheet and any special criteria from your construction contract with the information available from any plans and specifications of the project.

With these resources, continue dividing the project into its ordered parts to determine:

- How much work is required
- How big the crew will be
- How many worker-hours are needed for each task
- How many subcontractors are involved
- How you will schedule the work to best use your crew, equipment, and subcontractors.

Critical Scheduling Items in the Schedule

Critical items are those materials, supplies, and/or services that have to be ordered or planned well in advance of actual construction or installation. Critical items include:

- Specialty products with long order periods such as:

  - Appliances
  - Cabinets
  - Doors
  - Windows
  - Special moldings
  - Carpet
  - Fixtures; etc.

- Subcontractors that require more lead time for a project
- Weather sensitive installations and closures such as:

  - Roofing applications
  - Exterior painting procedures
  - Landscaping

"Have no fear of perfection - you'll never reach it."
Salvadore Dali

Most changes to your schedule will involve subcontractors and suppliers. If a subcontractor's schedule is altered by another project, or if a supplier gets a back-order on some item, changes have to be made. Your job is to learn of changes as soon as possible.

Crystal Ball

Sometimes knowing when to order and arrange for delivery of critical items is a "tricky" part of scheduling. Contractors often require the equivalent of a crystal ball to pinpoint the exact date a critical item may be needed.

By acknowledging that these items exist and will have to be dealt with in advance, you have already correctly read into the future.

A schedule lists events in a timely order, or chronologically. Many times an item has to be dealt with long before it is needed to go into place. Your schedule has to list the date for ordering so the item is ready for installation on time.

Controlling The Process

As a general contractor, you are responsible for the success of a project. You are the captain of the team and often the only one who knows the entire game plan for the project.

While keeping the scope of the project in mind, you also have to pay close attention to all the small details.

Small Details

Ignoring any of the many small details of a project can be a primary cause for delay. The small details that you should pay attention to include:

- The color and style of the roofing material
- The exact manner in which the corners will be trimmed on the siding
- The finish texture on the drywall
- The style and color of doorknobs
- The placement and type of electrical switches and outlets throughout the project

Decisions, Decisions, Decisions

These aesthetic details are important to the scheduling process because each choice of color, texture or style represents a decision the owner and designer both have to make.

The act of ordering certain materials and supplies depends on these cosmetic decisions. As the person with the entire project in mind, it is up to you to anticipate the decision making process and keep the project moving.

Details, Details, Details

When you think of it, a construction project is built on details. Not only are there numerous cosmetic decisions, but each person connected with the project requires unique preparations and decisions to finish their part of the project.

If you wait until you are sure your project will come out perfectly, you are likely to wait a very long time.

As a general contractor, you need specific details particular to the project from the following parties:

- The architect or designer
- The owner
- Your work crew
- Subcontractors
- Suppliers

This includes, but is not limited to:

- Work item numbers
- Item descriptions

- Units of measurement (cubic yard, square foot, pound, ton, each, etc.)
- Quality of work to be performed (specification standard)
- Relation of each item to the whole in terms of work to be performed (such as percentage of the total work required for each item)
- Units of time used in the schedule (days, hours)
- Starting date
- Time required for each item
- Completion date

Staying Organized

Staying organized means that you are keeping track of all these details and taking the extra time to write down the decisions for all the details. Keeping the details of a project tightly organized is the only way to guarantee a smooth flowing project. This means you'll have a project that is:

- More efficient
- Likely to be completed on time
- Able to be completed within the budget

Note
You can never be too organized. Organization takes extra time. However, the time you spend organizing is more than repaid the first time you have to track down a detail that you "know you have somewhere." Organization reflects your professionalism.

Scheduling should be boring; that is, no surprises. Good routines produce solid schedules.

Progress Reports

Progress reports are a special ingredient in the formula for a successful scheduling system. They are the best way to monitor the progress of the project. A progress report helps a general contractor perform three basic steps in monitoring a project:

- Comparing actual progress against the planned schedule
- Finding the cause of any difference between actual and scheduled progress
- Taking immediate action to either correct, balance, or reschedule activities to stay on, or close to, the original schedule

Daily Reports

Some general contractors request daily progress reports from their supervisor or employees and all subcontractors. A daily report provides a continuous, running check on the progress of the project. A daily report is useful to describe work to be done the following workday.

Progress reports help everyone keep up-to-date on their part of the project. As a general contractor, you can keep everyone on the project reporting progress to you through these daily reports.

Completion Reports

Another popular way to track progress is to monitor production rate. Naturally, this only lends itself well to work that easily shows measurable progress or can be measured by the worker-hour, number of bricks laid, or squares of roofing installed, for example.

People in the field know the most about the day-to-day progress and problems of a project. You are not likely to know the most about your projects unless you have way to debrief the field people. The sooner you know about problems, the better.

Time standards have been developed for certain construction activities and are found in time estimating books. These books are similar to the ones an auto mechanic would use to price work.

However, construction work is best calculated by the experienced workers and contractors who can keep you up-do-date. Your best long-term strategy is to know for yourself the time it takes to complete most projects. Use the expertise of your subcontractors to estimate the time it takes to complete those parts of the project that you are unfamiliar with.

Actual worker-hour totals can be compared against your estimates. Keep records of project time totals for your own use in scheduling. Tailor a method that enables you to collect enough information to catch problems early, but does not make reporting information an obstacle.

Anticipate Problems

Anticipate problems that may affect the project such as:

- Adverse weather conditions

- Vacations for employees and subcontractors
- Specific deadlines of owners or suppliers
- Unusually difficult aspects of the project for workers

Project Control Element	What Might Go Wrong?	How and When Will I Know?	What Can Be Done About It?
Project Time Line	1. Weather Delay 2. Roofing Sub	Watch Weather Report Confirm When Available	Prepare For Cover Dry-in Roof Ourselves
Project Budget Amount	Finish Labor on Staircase	When Finish Carpenter Makes Firm Bid After Rough Finish	Negotiate to Hold to First Estimate
Project Quality Issue	Drywall on Tallwall and Vaulted Ceiling	When Sun Shines Through Skylights on Finished Joists	Talk to Drywall Sub About Joints on Wall and Ceiling

Alternatives

Sometimes, no matter how well you plan, schedule, and monitor, delays come up. In this case, the schedule may have to be pushed back.

When the schedule requires major adjustment, be certain that all those affected are informed promptly with a written progress report.

Notify all the affected parties, such as owners, subcontractors, architects, suppliers, loan institutions, and the owners of the next construction project, that you are experiencing a delay.

Dispute Resolution

Schedule conflicts with owners and subcontractors may arise when drastic, or even moderate changes are necessary in a project. It is important to develop good negotiation skills to resolve these conflicts.

Residential Construction Outline

"Experience is the name everyone gives to their mistakes."
Oscar Wilde

This section contains a general construction flow outline. Not all residential projects necessarily proceed in the same sequence. In addition, this outline is not detailed enough to be a Project Breakdown and Duration Checklist as described in Chapter 3: "Scheduling Systems."

This outline can, and should be used as a reference when you formulate a checklist and set up a schedule for residential projects.

Preliminary Work

- Obtain the necessary building permits. Do not start construction without them.
- Site mapping. Locate and mark any items on the site for which special care will be required. This could include the following items:

    - Underground utilities such as:

        - Sewer lines
        - Electrical lines
        - Irrigation lines

    - Trees and vegetation that have to be preserved.

- Contact the servicing power company to install a temporary powerpole and hook up the electricity. If this is not to be done, make other arrangements for electricity for your power tools.
- Arrange for water hook up, temporary or otherwise. This means contacting the plumber and coordinating with public utilities. Permanent water hook up is not done until after foundation walls are constructed.
- Construct a shed to store tools and equipment.

Construction Process

- Begin transit work and project layout. This can include setting up batter boards, stakes, and strings.
- Begin excavation by removing topsoil you can save for later use. The excavator prepares the site according to

the plans and the transit layout. Included in this process is:

◆ Preparing footing trenches.
◆ Excavating the basement if required.
◆ Completing other trenchwork, including drainlines, sewer/waste water management, etc.

Payment schedules equal project schedules. If the project schedule is on time, payments can be on time. If payments slow or come to a stop because of delays in the project, cash flow can suffer greatly. Slow cash flow is one of a contractor's greatest causes of failure.

■ Complete form work and steel reinforcement work. This may happen in stages or as one large production. This depends on whether the footings and stem-walls are going to be laid separately or as a monolithic pour.

Inspection: Check forms before pouring concrete.

■ Footings and foundation walls are completed by the concrete contractor.
■ Proper curing time has to be allowed before forms are removed and other construction begins.
■ The plumber and electrician have to install any subsoil pipe lines and/or conduit.
■ Draintile (perforated pipe) is installed around footings.
■ Drainpipes have to be laid to handle water from gutters.

How can I make scheduling "brainless"? How can scheduling become routine enough that those involved can follow routines without "remembering".

More and more suppliers are being forced to set firm delivery schedules so that materials and supplies are at the project site on time and as needed. Find out what a supplier can do about delivery on all your orders.

Inspection: Underground installations such as pipelines, draintile, and conduit have to be inspected before backfilling.

■ Any waterproofing of the exterior of the foundation walls has to be done before backfilling occurs.
■ Backfilling around the foundation is now possible. However, the decision to do it now or after framing is up to the contractor.

There is often a need for access to the subsurface area around the footings (maybe another waterline needs to be run). For this and other reasons it is not always desirable to backfill at such an early date.

If backfilling is delayed until after framing, the workers have to contend with working around excavation piles. This means walking across planks, and setting ladders and scaffolds from within the foundation trench. Risk of injury is greatly increased when having to work around such obstacles.

In addition, working under these conditions (especially in wet weather) increases the time to complete framing and other activities.

- Start floor framing.
- Install any "rough" plumbing, electrical, and mechanical work.

Inspection: Check plumbing, electrical, and mechanical work before covering up.

Clean-up: Schedule a general underfloor cleanup.

- Install underfloor insulation. (Assuming, a wood frame floor.)

Inspection: Check insulation and floor framing before covering with subflooring.

A happy customer is an informed customer, even when things are going bad.

- Frame the wall, ceiling, and roof. Be sure to schedule time for straightening and bracing walls before ceiling joists and trusses are installed.
- Build chimney and fireplace after rough framing has been completed.
- Rough-in plumbing, electrical, and mechanical work can occur as soon as basic "dry-in" has been accomplished, (the roofing felt or actual roofing has been applied.)
- Frame exterior doors, windows, and do other special framing during rough-in work.

Inspection: Check all rough-in work and framing before covering up with drywall or anything else.

Clean-up: Schedule a clean-up.

- Install insulation.

Inspection: Check wall and attic insulation before covering.

■ Drywall or plaster contractor installs wallboard. Schedule time to apply heat ventilation to dry out the structure. This is especially true if:

    ♦ Nails are used instead of screws to hang wall board
    ♦ Green, instead of kiln-dried lumber is used for walls and ceilings
    ♦ There has been wet weather

If it weren't for the last minute a lot less would get done.

In many cases a permit may not be required. Repairs and replacements of roofing, siding, windows, painting and floorcovering are some examples. Remember that you could lose valuable legal rights if work is done without a permit, when required, and there is a problem.

Clean-up: Plastering is messy business. This is a good time to schedule a cleanup.

Inspection: The installation of wall (and ceiling) board will have to be inspected prior to applying "mud."

■ Continue exterior carpentry during the drying and plastering process.
■ If a basement exists, complete the concrete basement floor before interior finish work.

Clean-up: Clean up scraps made during exterior carpentry.

■ Painters apply primary and base coat where feasible after drywall or plaster has fully dried, (The painter may have already moved in to pre-paint items such as windows and doors.)
■ Complete the interior. The sequence of the interior work activities is typically in the following order:

    ♦ Underlayment
    ♦ Unfinished wood flooring
    ♦ Interior door frames are hung
    ♦ Wood paneling
    ♦ Cabinets
    ♦ Interior trim, including door and window trim, and most other trim work

> *Note*
>
> Baseboard and base shoe may be held off until applying finish flooring. Typically, baseboard is applied before carpeting. However, the need to do painting touch-up should be expected.

- Painters are typically on the project on a regular basis at this point. Weather permitting, they can be doing outside work while inside carpentry is happening. They could also be pre-finishing interior trim before it is applied.
- Complete tile work at this time. Decide exactly when this work should be scheduled. For example, tile work in a bath could be the last activity. However, paint jobs on walls and cabinets are subject to damage. If the tile work is scheduled first, schedule time for proper curing.
- Finish electrical work, such as:

    - Installing final switches and outlets
    - Installing cover plates
    - Hanging fixtures

- Finish plumbing. This includes installation of:

    - Sinks
    - Faucets
    - Showerheads
    - Toilets

- Finish flooring, carpeting especially, is best done last. The same is true for applying the finish coats of urethane to wood floors.
- In certain cases this is not possible. For example, the finish flooring needs to be installed in the bathrooms before the plumber can set the toilet.

Inspection: Check to see if the nailing of the underlayment has to be inspected before covering with finish flooring. If so, schedule an inspection.

- Finish grade the exterior while the interior is being completed. Install concrete flat-work, such as sidewalks and driveways. Consider if any of this work will affect entering or exiting the building.

Project scheduling is a key part of construction management. It can also be considered part of the company administration or doing your "contractor work".

Inspection: As with the foundation, check forms and steel work before pouring concrete for sidewalks and driveways.

Clean-up: Schedule at least two substantial clean-ups during the finishing process.

- Landscaping is often the final process of the construction project. However, final grading sometimes has to happen before pouring sidewalks and driveways.

Clean-up: Schedule a final clean-up. Make sure that the windows and house are as clean as possible and that all scrap material has been removed.

- Schedule a final inspection, after which a Certificate of Occupancy is issued.

You can promote better scheduling if you build in bonuses and penalties with your subcontractors. On time, or ahead-of-schedule, performance means a bonus. A delay means a penalty. Your bargaining factor in this type of arrangement is your prompt payment. People will do a lot for you in exchange for prompt payment.

Summary

This chapter has discussed the importance of scheduling for completing a project in a timely manner. Some of the important factors to remember are:

- Organization is the key to success in scheduling. As a general contractor, you have to manage all the pieces of the project. Your organizing skills are critical to the success of a scheduling system.
- Being realistic in what can be done. There is no point in setting a schedule that cannot be maintained. Your information about the worker's and subcontractor's ability to keep up with your schedule has to be accurate.
- Do not overlook waiting periods and inspection requirements. Your schedule has to include all of the pieces of the project. Be sure to identify all waiting times and required inspections.

"The world is moving so fast these days that the man who says it can't be done is generally interupted by someone doing it." Harrey Emerson Fusdick

Exhibit 1: Estimate/Cost Summary

Estimate/Cost Summary

Owner: _____

Address: _____

Today's Date:_____ Projected Start: _____ Finish:_____

Item	Material	Labor	Subs.	Total	Actual $
Permits					
Plans					
Excavation					
Demolition/Removal					
Concrete					
Forms					
Insulation					
Masonry					
Rough Carpentry					
Decks or Detached					
Finish Carpentry					
Roofing					
Flooring					
Plumbing					
Heating					
Sheet Metal					
Electrical					
Plaster/Drywall					
Paint and Decorating					
Glass and Glazing					
Cabinets					
Ceramic Tile					
Counter Tops					
Appliances					
Equipment Rental					
Clean Up					
Light Fixture Allowance					
Finish Hardware Allowance					
Bath Hardware Allowance					
Doors Including Garage					
Total Direct Cost					
Markup					
Grand Total					
Extras					

Exhibit 2: Project Specifications

Project Specifications

Contractor's Name
Address
City _____ **State** ____ **Zip** _____
Phone _____
Prepared by _____

Contractor proposes to provide the building permit, labor, materialsand equipment necessary to complete installation of the following:

Construction Requirements   Description
Removal _____
Addition _____
Other: _____

Plumbing Requirements Description
Removal _____
Supply _____

Walls
Removal _____
Tub area _____
Other _____

Ceilings
Removal _____
Finish _____
Other _____

Ventilating
Fan _____
Venting _____
Other _____

Accessories   Finish   Number   Description
Matched tile _____
Tub trim _____
Other _____

Heating/Cooling
Heating _____
Size _____
Other _____

Electrical & Lighting
Removal _____
Service entrance _____
Other _____

Tops (   ) As per drawing attached
Material _____
Style _____
Other _____

Owner's Name
Address
City _____ **State** ____ **Zip** _____
Job Address _____
Phone _____
Date _____ **Job No.** _____
Waste _____
Steam _____

Floor
Removal _____
Other _____

Medicine Cabinet(s)
Quantity _____
Other _____

Fixtures & Fittings Color Description Cost
Tub _____
Other _____

Vanity No. 1   Vanity No. 2
Cabinet style _____
Other _____

Enclosures
Description _____
Other _____

Storage
Type _____
Other _____

Lavatories
Quantity _____
Other _____

Contractor will do the following demolition and dispose of items removed:

❑ Vanity   ❑ Top   ❑ Lavatory   ❑ Tub   ❑ Commode
❑ Shower enclosure   ❑ Radiator   ❑ Medicine Cabinet
❑ Bath fittings   ❑ Deteriorated pipe   ❑ Flooring

Contractor will make the following repairs:
Item   Description

_____

Owner will furnish labor and material as follows:
Item   Description

_____

These are the total and complete specifications for this job. Only the items checked or for which a cost is indicated are included in this job.

Contractor _____ Owner _____
Date _____

Exhibit 3: Proposal and Agreement

Proposal and Agreement

Date: _____ Contractor: _____

Address: _____ Phone: _____

Agreement with: _____

Project Address: _____

The undersigned agrees to furnish materials, tools, equipment and supplies, and to execute in a substantial and workmanlike manner according to accepted trade practices the following listed work on the property noted above:

_____

_____

_____

_____

_____

_____

The following listed documents are a part of this agreement:

The following items are specifically excluded from this agreement and are to be furnished by others or treated as additional work:

Allowances: The following amounts are included as allowances for the items listed. In event costs are less than an allowance the difference shall be credited to the Owner. If costs are more than an allowance the Contractor shall be reimbursed the excess.

Light fixtures and chimes: _____ $_____ .

Finish hardware: _____ $_____ .

Bath accessories: _____ $_____ .

Item: _____ $_____ .

Item: _____ $_____ .

Note: Finish hardware is interpreted to include all knobs, pulls, hinges, catches, locks, drawer slides, accessories or other items that are normally installed subsequent to final painting. Light fixtures are interpreted to include only those that are surface-mounted. Bath accessories are interpreted to include medicine cabinets, towel bars, paper holders, soap dishes, etc.

In consideration for materials, labor, and services specified above, Owner agrees to pay Contractor the sum of $_____ to be payable as follows: $_____ upon signing of this agreement; the balance in this manner:

As Owner's failure to make prompt payments will cause a financial hardship on the Contractor, it is necessary to impose a finance charge if payments are not promptly made. Accordingly, Owner agrees to pay a finance charge on amounts not paid within 30 days based on the rate of 1½ per month, or an annual rate of 18%.

Contractor agrees to commence work on or about _____ and to diligently pursue work through to completion. Completion to be approximately _____.
(Please note #7 of the "General Conditions")

In view of changing labor and material conditions, this agreement is subject to review unless accepted in writing and this or other mutually acceptable agreement is signed within 30 days of date above.

By: _____

Contractor's Name: _____ Business #: _____

Acceptance:
Contractor is authorized to proceed with the work listed in this agreement according to the terms and conditions on the reverse side hereof, which are acknowledged as part of this agreement.

Date: _____   _____

_____

Terms and Conditions of Contract

1. **PROTECTION OF OWNER'S PROPERTY.** Owner agrees to remove or to protect any personal property, inside and out, including shrubs and flowers which cannot be protected adequately by contractor, and contractor shall not be held responsible for damage to or loss of said items.

2. **PERMITS.** Contractor shall obtain and pay for all permits required by government bodies unless otherwise specified. Owner shall gain approval from any group, association, or society which may have to approve the project as part of a prior covenant.

3. **TERMITE WORK.** Contractor shall not be obligated to perform any work to correct damage caused by termites or dry rot unless noted specifically in agreement.

4. **PROPERTY LINES.** Owner shall furnish, at their expense, evidence of property lines and is responsible for their accuracy unless otherwise agreed to.

5. **FILLED GROUND, ROCK OR SPRINGS.** In the event filled ground is encountered or rock (or any other material not removable by ordinary hand tools), owner shall pay cost plus 18% contractor's fee. If springs are encountered they will be dealt with at owner's expense after discussion with building inspector and owner.

6. **ACCESS TO WORK.** Owner agrees to grant free access to work areas for workers and vehicles, and designate areas for storage of materials and rubbish. Owner shall take care to keep driveways clear for parking during work hours. Contractor agrees to take care to protect property of owner and adjacent property but shall not be responsible for damage to driveways, shrubs, lawns, trees, or movement of trucks unless due to gross negligence of contractor. Contractor agrees to secure repair for any damage caused by workers on the project and return the landscape as close to the original as possible. Owner agrees to take into consideration time of year and condition of soil for the reasonableness of the finish grade.

7. **INSURANCE.** Prior to commencement of construction, Owner shall have Contractor listed as loss-payee on fire and comprehensive insurance policy by means of endorsement and shall furnish waiver of subrogation for fire and those items covered under comprehensive policy including vandalism; or shall purchase separate policy to protect Contractor's interests. In event Owner fails to do so, Contractor may procure such insurance and Owner agrees to reimburse Contractor in cash for the cost thereof. Contractor shall carry at his own expense workmen's compensation and public liability insurance at least to the minimum requirements of existing laws.

8. **TOILET FACILITIES.** Owner agrees to make toilet facilities available to all workers or compensate Contractor for cost of rented units.

9. **ELECTRICAL SERVICE.** Contractor does not include the cost of changing electrical service unless specifically noted in agreement. The determination of what is to be done to provide the most efficient electrical service is the responsibility of the electrical sub-contractor.

10. **UNDERGROUND PIPES.** Contractor shall not be held responsible for damage to, or removing of pipes, sprinkler lines, water or sewage disposal systems or conduits in areas of excavation, grading, paving or construction. Contractor agrees to take all reasonable care to protect those specific underground items that are pointed out and located by markers by the owner.

11. **DAMAGE TO PROPERTY.** Contractor shall not be held responsible for damages caused by owner or owner's agent or owner's employees, act of god, soil slippage, earthquake, fire, riot, civil commotion or acts of public enemy.

12. **MATERIALS REMOVED - RUBBISH.** All materials removed from the project during the course of alterations will be disposed of by the contractor except those items designated by the owner prior to the construction commencement. The project will be kept clean to the extent reasonable for the conditions, and the premises will be left broom clean prior to departing the project. Owner agrees to inform contractor prior to start of construction if there be any other requirements for cleanliness and to compensate if they be other than above.

13. **EXTRA TIME.** Contractor agrees to diligently pursue the timely completion of the project. Owner agrees not to hold contractor responsible for delays due to the following; acts of neglect or omission by the owner or owner's employees or agents, acts of god, stormy or inclement weather, strikes, lockouts, boycotts, or other labor union activities, and further that any delays caused by inspections, corrections, or changes ordered by owner are included.

14. **WORK STOPPAGE.** Should the project be stopped by any public authority for a period of thirty days or more, through no fault of the contractor, or should the work be halted by an act or because of neglect of the owner for a period of fifteen days, or should the owner fail to pay the contractor any payment within fifteen days after it is due, then the contractor upon seven days written notice to the owner may stop work or terminate the contract and recover from the owner payment for all work completed and any loss sustained plus reasonable profit and damages.

15. **EXTRA WORK.** Should the owner desire to add items to be done after the start of construction, the amount for such extra work will be determined in advance if possible. If not determined in advance the owner agrees to pay contractor for actual cost of labor and materials plus 18% contractor's fee. All sums for extra work are payable at completion of the work requested. This item is not to be confused with a change order which is reduced to writing and involves deviations from the plans and specifications of the original agreement.

16. **MATCHING MATERIALS.** Contractor calls to the owner's attention that there sometimes are limitations in the ability to match plaster, stucco, concrete, masonry and roofing material. Although contractor will make every effort to match textures, colors, and planes, exact duplication is not promised.

17. **LICENSING.** Contractor informs owner that the company is licensed under the laws and statutes of this state or with a local agency.

18. **CANCELLATION OF AGREEMENT.** In the event of the cancellation of this agreement by the owner prior to start of construction the contractor shall be compensated by the owner for all expenses incurred to that date plus five percent of the contract price as liquidated damages and not as a penalty.

19. **LIENS AND ASSESSMENTS.** Contractor shall not be held responsible for any bonds, liens or assessments on existing real estate belonging to owner, nor to any sewer or utility assessment not yet a lien on the owner's property.

20. **SIGN.** Contractor is authorized to display his or her sign in a tasteful manner during the course of the project.

21. **CONTRACT.** The owner is not to sign the agreement in blank and will be offered a copy at the time it is signed.

22. **GUARANTEE.** All work done in the course of fulfilling this agreement and that work designated as extra or done under a change order is guaranteed for one year following substantial completion. Those items guaranteed by the manufacturer are covered by their written warranty. Full payment to contractor must precede these guarantees. Contractor makes clear his intent to diligently and promptly respond to make necessary repairs and corrections to work performed.

23. **NOTICE TO OWNER.** Materials, supplies and labor are being provided by contractor pursuant to the owner-contractor agreement. Contractor is entitled to place a lien against your property under Construction Lien Laws as described by state law.

Chapter 2

Dealing with Others on the Project

One of the greatest personal assets a contractor can develop is good communication skills. Add the energy to put such a skill to work for the benefit of your project, and you have a strong business advantage.

Communication is the information "wiring" of the contracting business. It is the means by which every phase of the contracting process is connected to every other phase.

More and more professional remodel contractors use a lead carpenter for their crew. This person is in charge of the project from the start until it is ready for finish work. The lead person builds a relationship with you to solve problems and keep the project going.

Each construction project requires a communication network that reaches all the persons and businesses that are involved with the project.

The contractor is the master "electrician" who "splices" together this communication network. The project schedule is the main "service panel" through which the information that is vital to the project flows.

I can only please one person per day. Today is not your day. Tomorrow isn't looking good either.

Although many people see construction contracting as simply building things, contractors may spend one-third to one-half of their time simply interacting and dealing with:

- Owners
- Employees
- Subcontractors
- Architects, designers, and engineers
- Suppliers
- Inspectors

Contractors often find themselves hammering phone numbers

rather than nails. Keeping the lines of communication open frequently becomes the contractors day and evening pastime.

Establish a Communication Process

As the general contractor, you have the greatest responsibility for getting your project done on time and within budget. There are a few communication procedures you can use to help yourself be a successful project coordinator. Some initial communication procedures you may want to use are:

- A pre-project meeting
- A preliminary schedule of the project
- Gaining input from tradespeople who will work on the project

"Drive thy business or it will drive thee."
Benjamin Franklin

Pre-project Meeting

The pre-project meeting provides a time and place where all major parties associated with the project can meet and discuss the flow of activities (schedule) for the project. This meeting can establish a mutual understanding of the scope of the project and identify potential scheduling problems.

It is best to schedule this meeting after the contract is signed and within a few weeks of starting the project.

Meeting Goals

Setting the stage for smooth completion of the work schedule is the primary goal of the pre-project meeting.

In this meeting, all the people who have substantial involvement with the project should express their concerns and needs. Such interaction has a positive effect on how smoothly the project will run.

In some cases, where you are trying to meet a start up time goal, you can get an inspection of footing and stem walls while the plans are being reviewed. A building official may allow an early inspection to occur to get the project going, especially if coming weather is an issue. Normally this is for footing and foundation walls only, and then only after zoning issues and lot issues are settled.

Introducing the Involved Parties

"Lots of folks confuse bad management with destiny."
Kim Hubbard

One of the functions of the pre-project meeting is to introduce the primary people involved in the project to each other. This is especially important for the owners. Owners normally want to know who will be on the project.

The meeting is also a good place to prepare the owners for what to expect during the construction. Unrealistic expectations can be identified and discussed in an effort to prevent major surprises later.

Each primary person in the project can discuss issues of their part of the project with the owners. In this meeting the owners and subcontractors can determine how specific problems with dust, noise, parking, debris removal and securing the owners property may be handled.

Preliminary Schedule

Develop a preliminary schedule for the project. This preliminary schedule can serve as an agenda for your pre-project meeting.

Many contractors use a calander to show projects that are contracted and pending. This chart shows general work activity and will keep you from stacking too much work in a month. It also allows you to decline some work that is not as profitable when you have a surplus of projects pending.

The preliminary schedule is an outline of the major parts of the project. It includes start and finish times, major points in the project such as foundation, framing complete, dry in, project secured, and times the owner may have to vacate the project.

Use Your Estimate Sheet

Use your estimate sheet and other project documents, such as the contract, plans, and specifications, to develop a preliminary schedule. (A more detailed description of schedule development will be laid out in Chapter 3: "Scheduling Systems.")

Communicating The Schedule

The main benefit of early communication is finding out where potential scheduling conflicts are.

This is a critical part of the scheduling process. You will have to know that key parts of the project can be done on time to avoid other problems. Examples of this are:

- Can the plumber be on the project as soon as the post and beams are installed?
- Will the cabinets be finished by the painter right after they are installed?
- What other outside work can be scheduled while the inside part of the project is restricted to one activity, such as painting or floor covering?
- Will the appliances be delivered by the suppliers just before the electrician arrives on the project to install them?

Scheduling problems are bound to surface in this shaking out stage. Some things to keep in mind are:

- Scheduling problems will not go away by themselves.
- Scheduling problems require attention, consideration, and resolution.
- Scheduling problems require communication. It may seem that ignoring clients and co-workers buys time when, in fact, problems will usually become larger.

Soliciting Input

Present this preliminary schedule to those at the meeting. (Also, send copies to those who could not attend.) Explain that the schedule is only preliminary. You want to solicit input from others, especially owners and subcontractors.

Be certain that all the critical parts of the project are covered in the preliminary schedule, such as:

- Notifying subcontractors of their timing on the project
- Noting on the schedule where inspections are required
- Warning the owner in a remodel project when work will be noisy or especially dirty so they can be gone during that time
- Noting when, during the course of the project, you will or will not be present on the project site

Irate owner, "You told me that this bath remodel would only take 10 days, start to finish." "But I didn't mean in a row" the contractor said.

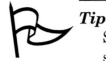

Tip
Strongly encourage all those involved in the project to suggest changes and revisions to your preliminary schedule. After all, the reason these tradespeople were chosen for the project was, in large part, because of their expertise.

Taking Notes

Take written notes of what people say. Make special notations regarding possible schedule conflicts or criteria stated by the owners and the subcontractors. Be sure to write these notes out and distribute the new information to everyone who has to know about it.

The All Purpose Tool

Remember that scheduling is more than just determining who shows up and when they show up on the project. It is also a tool that:

- Outlines the total project plan based on time factors that affect labor
- Outlines the process for getting each phase of the project done and ordering materials and products for each phase of the project
- Outlines and tracks the flow of money through the project, such as progress payments and billings from subcontractors and suppliers
- Helps determine when inspections will be needed
- Helps monitor the progress or lack of progress on the project
- Equalizes the work activity to reduce labor and material waste
- Communicates with the primary people on the project

Your customer has a schedule too. They are relying on your promise of completion for a next step. Make sure your customer isn't putting too much pressure on you by setting your completion date to close to the date they want to start the next step.

Working with Owners

There are at least five aspects to the construction project you need to address when working with the owners of the project:

- Inconvenience to them caused by the project
- Safety and security of both them and the property
- The owner's role in the decision making process

- Technical aspects of the project
- Financial aspects of the project

Quality can be managed and controlled. You have to change the conditions in some cases to hold a quality situation. Add time, or add people, to stay in a quality mode. The project schedule has to account for these variations.

Describing the Inconvenience

The primary concerns are inconvenience, interference, and conflict that construction activities have over normal family or office activities.

Many times owners base their satisfaction of how the project went for them not on the actual results of the building process, but on their perceived degree of convenience or inconvenience during construction.

This is especially true for remodel projects, but it is also true for new construction. Owners involved in new custom home construction will be very busy with the project. They appreciate the efforts of an organized contractor as much as the remodel owner appreciates a well planned project.

The success of a project depends on its schedule. The project schedule is the road map for managers and workers. Owners have a right to expect the schedule to be correct, unless notified. Keep in touch!

Points To Consider

There are many points to consider. To identify areas of inconvenience to owners, here are a few regarding the owner's convenience:

- Special health or other requirements (access for example) of a family member or office worker
- Special routines or schedules of the family or office
- Daily work time windows (how early, late, or long you may work)
- The possibility of working weekends
- Neighbors who are day sleepers
- Neighbors who may be offended for other reasons (dust, noise, general disarray)

The main idea is to accommodate the family or office staff and those they care about or have to impress. After all, it is their home or work environment. Each project situation has its own priorities and requirements.

If you can work it out with your clients, you can schedule "pick-up" work when a schedule breaks down. You are certain to have call-backs and repairs on various projects. Keep these jobs on hold until a schedule allows someone to do the work. Most of the time your client will help you out by being flexible about this work.

Setting Expectations

One family may not care what the house or yard looks like as long as company can make it through the door. Another family may want to keep the back yard open and available for the children to play.

For each family or office, there are different preferences. Look for opportunities to keep your customer happy.

Major Interruptions

Certain construction operations require that people leave the construction area. Major plumbing or electrical operations may take a few days and it may be easier for the family to stay elsewhere.

While these are major inconveniences, it is by far better to let the owner know well ahead of time so both the owner and you can schedule what each is to do. You do not want to have the subcontractor show up expecting the house or office to be vacant when it is not. This simply leads to more scheduling problems.

Safety and Security

Reassure the owners that you will keep their issues of project safety and security a priority during construction. Discuss the degree of focus necessary for the well-being of children and/or pets on or near the construction site.

A schedule is a guide. Don't let your schedule seem like a promise to the owner.

Another point to discuss with the owner is protection of valuable items. Valuables should be protected from theft and damage during the construction process by the owner.

Theft and damage are issues relatively common to construction sites. If you are in a location that demands special attention to issues of safety and security, your cost estimate and project schedule have to reflect that.

Note
If you have further interest, see the *Advantage Contractor Business Success Series* course, *Project Site Safety and Security for Construction Contractors.*

Making Decisions

It is critical for scheduling that owners make prompt and timely decisions throughout the project. Be certain that you clearly communicate to the owners that this is part of their "project description." Part of your job as a contractor is to develop the project schedule with these timely decisions by the owners in mind.

Along with the architect or designer, you have to inform the owners, well in advance, when decisions by them will be necessary.

Relating Technical Aspects

Sometimes the owner does not understand the technical aspects of their building project and may see your efforts as a waste. Keeping everyone informed keeps communication open and will go a long way toward preventing such disputes.

A good policy is to introduce the owner to the subcontractors if the subcontractors were not present at the pre-project meeting.

Questions and Answers

Before construction begins, make sure the owners have a chance to ask questions about any aspect they are uncomfortable with or do not understand. Then, after dealing with any issues brought up, assure the owners that they can call you during construction with questions they may have about any part of the project.

"It is not enough to have a good mind. The main thing is to use it well."
Rene Descartes

The Construction Contract

Your contract with the owner is the appropriate place to formally (in writing) address issues of possible project delays. Many standardized contract clauses (known as "boilerplate" terms and conditions) specify that the contractor is not responsible for delays in the project due to "Acts of God" or "Concealed Conditions." See Exhibit 3, p. 21-23.

The contract sets out your promises to the owner. Now is not the time to change your mind on what is supposed to happen on the project site.

Other clauses might specify which party is responsible for the cost of stolen or vandalized property, or materials and supplies associated with the project.

Even more critical to scheduling are those clauses dealing with rewards for damages the owner may be entitled to if the project delay is your fault.

Your construction contract should also deal with change order situations. When the scope of the project is altered (work added or deleted) it affects the cost of the project as well as the schedule.

Warning

If your construction contract does not address the previous issues, you should be concerned that your business interests may not be adequately protected. Acquire the knowledge necessary to develop a valid and adequate construction contract.

Regardless of whether these issues are or are not a part of your contract document, they still have to be reviewed or discussed when making the project schedule.

In the course of selling, scheduling and collecting payments for your project, the terms of various contracts come into play. Your contract with the owner will set start and finish dates. The subcontractors will have start and finish dates. The schedule has to stay in line with these demands to collect payments on time; all the contract terms have to flow together.

Take this a step further by reviewing specific items that will be installed. Make sure that the owner understands that the contract specifies certain:

- Materials will be used in specific applications
- Fixtures named by type and model
- Floor coverings described by pattern and manufacturer
- Finish materials to be installed by name and size

Review each specification to be certain that the owner understands the specifications.

Financial Considerations

Last but not the least of your scheduling (and contract) concerns, is the issue of prompt and timely progress payments.

Your project schedule will have to coordinate payments for the work performed to materials ordered. Discuss issues of payment with the owners, especially how the contract may require advance payments. Have this discussion before the work starts. Use the schedule you have worked out to show the owners the importance of timely payments.

Next to a stop work order from the local building department, nothing will shut a project down faster than lack of funds to pay those doing the work or supplying the materials.

Some owners will want speed at all costs. If you are up to it, and the extra money is worth it, go for it. This is not for the faint of heart.

Employees

When developing a schedule, you have to estimate how long each part of the project will take. This normally depends on how many workers there will be performing each task.

There are two less obvious, but equally crucial, relationships between your employees and your scheduling process:

- The scheduled work load needs to match the employee's ability to complete work on time.
- The employees should not overstep their authority by making agreements for you with the owner.

Load = Ability

One of the toughest scheduling (and cost estimating) tasks is to determine how many hours of labor it takes to finish a project.

There are many variables which have to be considered such as:

- Site conditions. Will workers have to contend with mud or icy surfaces?
- Physical conditions. Is the job physically difficult; such as high ladder work, or crawl space work?
- Technical aspects. Will the work require substantial calculations such as complex roof framing or stair building?
- Detail intensity. Is the work rough or finish in nature?

■ Transition periods. Will there be waiting periods for the paint to dry or the grout to set?

Besides the above variables, you also have to consider the skill level of your employee(s). You will have to be realistic when scheduling daily work loads.

Your project site lead person or supervisor is the direct link from you to the owner. Make it easy for everyone to communicate.

Laws of Nature

There is no substitute for experience in estimating how long a task will take. But experience is often not enough. There seems to be certain ancient and universal laws that govern almost all construction work. These "laws" also have to be considered when calculating how much work is possible for a given period of time.

One of these "laws" is known as "Murphy's Law," which states that, "whatever can go wrong, will go wrong." The other "law" does not have a name but is just as notorious, it states, "the project will always take longer."

A general contractor not only needs to rely on experience but also upon wisdom as well. Although these laws do not dictate the nature of the entire construction process all the time, the wise contractor always keeps them in mind when scheduling and cost estimating.

Some contractors like to schedule a project from the back forward. In this way they are always thinking, "What comes before this?" By thinking of what has to be done before, they find more details to list.

Overstepping Authority

Unless otherwise directed, employees have to be careful not to make contractual promises on your behalf. They should not deviate from either the contract or the plan, regardless of what the homeowner asks or demands.

"Talk to Me"

Make sure that communication is always open between you and your employees, especially with regard to project work activities. Make it clear that you are open to suggestions and information regarding the project.

Have employees review the schedule with you to help determine the current status of the project and to see if adjustments are necessary for future planning.

Be sure to notify the owner in writing prior to the project what authority your employees have to alter the contract. It is best to state in the contract the process for all changes in the project.

"If error is corrected wherever it is recognized as such, the path of error is the path of truth."
Hans Reichenbach

Supervisors

Sooner or later you will be taking on multiple projects, or will have projects where schedules overlap. Consequently, you will not be able to be available to both project sites at the same time.

You may have to put someone in charge while you are away from the project site. Finding a good supervisor, lead worker, or superintendent is just as important, if not more important, than finding good employees. The supervisor's leadership and management abilities could make or break your project.

Make sure your supervisor or lead person knows how to manage the activities on the project.

Workers

This combination of supervisors and employees comprise the project's work crew. How they work together is critical for your project's business and success.

You also have to keep them busy. You will only be able to do this through an accurate and thorough scheduling system. Constant layoffs and job uncertainty can lead to a breakdown in morale. Soon, employees may be jumping ship to find steadier work.

This is one reason to maintain a long term outlook and to be planning and scheduling one, two, or three months ahead. As your business grows, you may be planning six months or even a year ahead.

In setting the schedule for a project, you have to look at variables that affect time and quality of work. A work crew that is best for the project may be on another project for 3 weeks. The subcontractor you want is unavailable and the 2nd choice will go slower to produce the quality required. Distance from your office is a factor as well as other aspects of the site, such as grade and ease of getting around.

Long Range Planning and Scheduling

Long range planning is a key factor in the success of any business. Long range scheduling is simply an attempt to make schedules more specific.

Tip

Remember, business plans and schedules are not etched in stone. In fact, they are meant to be reviewed and revised continuously. A good schedule will be flexible.

A common dilemma for many contractors is finding enough time to develop a long range plan. However, there is an irony in this. Until the contractor schedules time for developing a long range plan, he or she may always be too busy for such important planning activities.

"The best thing about the future is that it comes only one day at a time."
Abraham Lincoln

Reviewing and revising your long range schedule helps you as a contractor to:

- Develop a plan for dealing with the seasonal business cycles of the construction business
- Determine financial strategies for dealing with these cycles
- Maintain an early warning system allowing you to effectively deal with problems as they emerge
- Maintain a dedicated work crew
- Establish a network of reliable subcontractors

It is nearly impossible to be too detailed. If you are to get each detail of the project into your schedule, you have to list it. You cannot assume anyone else will do something unless it is noted in the schedule at the correct point in the project.

Subcontractors

It is important to keep your subcontractors on schedule. General contracting, by definition, is developing a network of reliable subcontractors. When you find a good subcontractor, you have found someone you will want to develop an ongoing relationship with.

What makes a good subcontractor? This may seem like a simple question, but by giving this question some careful thought, you will establish criteria useful for evaluating the performance of present and future subcontractors.

Finding and Keeping Good Subcontractors

A subcontractor has to be:

- Someone who is legal. Does the subcontractor have a valid registration with the state licensing or registering agency? Does the person have proper workers' compensation coverage for employees? Can this contractor document current liability insurance and adequate bonding?

Tip

Have the subcontractor supply you with renewal dates for licensing or registration, bond, insurance, and any other required coverages.

- Someone you like. You have to be able to develop a working relationship with this person. Does the subcontractor share the same work ethic as you? If you do not like your subcontractors, the owners are not likely to either.
- Someone who is capable. Does proof exist that the subcontractor is capable of doing quality and efficient work? Check references and previous projects that the subcontractor has completed for this proof.
- Someone who is organized. Does the subcontractor demonstrate organized business procedures. Do they give:

  - Thorough written estimates
  - Itemized billings
  - Written schedules

- Someone with a track record of paying suppliers on time. An unpaid bill by a subcontractor for materials used on the project will give the supplier the right to place a lien on the property.
- Someone who is reasonably priced. The cheapest subcontractor is not always a good value. The super elite

It's your project. You got yourself into it. Do what has to be done, like it or not.

subcontractor may make your bids unaffordable to an owner.

- Someone who is willing to sign a subcontract. A subcontract is a sign of professionalism by the general and subcontractor. Do not work with a subcontractor who "doesn't need a subcontract."
- Someone who can communicate. Even the cheapest subcontractor who does the highest quality of work is not worth the frustration of not being reachable by phone or other means.
- Someone who is dependable. This means that the subcontractor does what is promised on time.
- Someone who will never leave you high and dry by not showing up on the project as promised.

"Neatness counts. Disorder multiplies." Dolores E. McGuire

This may seem like a demanding list but the construction business is a demanding business.

Warning

As the general contractor, you are ultimately responsible to the owner. Anything the subcontractor does, or does not do, affects your contractual duty to the owner.

Setting Mutual Expectations

Just as you expect high levels of performance and professionalism from your subcontractors, they expect the same high standards of your performance.

Subcontractor Scheduling

The time and work schedule for the subcontractors should show:

- Specific work to be done
- Names of the subcontractors doing each task
- Dates and times of work to be done by each subcontractor
- Notes for each subcontractor about the project

Ask Your Subcontractor

A good subcontractor is an expert in his or her specialty. Just as you rely on the subcontractor's expertise for calculating the cost of the project, you should do the same when setting up the schedule.

After you have developed your preliminary project schedule discuss it with the subcontractors. Ask them to carefully assess:

- The sequence of the schedule
- Any conflict with how their work has been inserted into the project
- The amount of time allotted
- Whether enough time has been reserved for their part of the project
- Any special requirements needed by the subcontractor that the schedule needs to address
- Any conflicts between the work activities of different contractors

It is impossible for a person to learn what they think they already know.

For example, will the plumber disconnect the water just as the plasterer needs to mix "mud."

Communication

Maintaining lines of communication with the subcontractor is always important. Remember, schedules are meant to be adjusted to new situations. You want a process in your scheduling system that enables you and your subcontractors (and others who may be affected) to routinely review and revise the schedule as necessary.

Progress Reports

Daily, weekly, or monthly progress reports are valuable tools for communicating with subcontractors and others associated with the project. Progress reports provide a form of documented communication. Having a record of your communications is helpful for future scheduling. Such records may also prove valuable when evidence relating to project delays is needed.

Notifying Your Subcontractor

In your progress reports you will want to discuss the difficulties each subcontractor may run into on the project, especially when two or more are working at the same time. For example, there could be an approaching scheduling problem if the plumber requires the water to be shut off at a time when another subcontractor needs water for something they are doing.

Major Source of Lost Time

One of the most common sources of scheduling problems is when the general contractor and the subcontractor are not on the same schedule. Usually both the general and subcontractor are working on multiple projects. Finding free time for the current project at the most useful time is critical.

Keeping In Touch

The general contractor should contact each subcontractor at least once a week, even if they're not working on the project. All parties benefit by knowing the status of the workers that are relative to the project at hand.

If anyone on the project gets behind, or ahead of schedule, there could be scheduling problems with all others. This coordination is critical to the success of your business.

Architects, Designers, and Engineers

Architects, designers and engineers often act as the owner's representative during construction of a project that they designed. Their role can be minor or major.

Minor Role Players

It took a while, but the snail reached the ark.

An architect's or designer's role may only be advisory. Any responsibility to the project may have ended when they received their final payment from the owner. In this case, consultation may only be necessary if a problem arises with the design or specifications of the project.

Major Role Players

On certain projects, especially large ones, the architect or designer may be the owner's representative on the project. Architects are most often assigned this role.

When an architect is involved, the construction contract may give the architect "third party approval" authority. Having such authority means that all work has to be approved by the architect or designer before the owner is obligated to pay the contractor.

When the architect has such authority, he or she is obligated by ethics and laws to "act in good faith." This means that he or she has to be fair and realistic in asserting this authority.

When the architect or designer plays a major roll in a project, you will want to consider the effect on your scheduling process.

Your entire company operation deals with scheduling. Input has to get to the correct place on time. How does your sales staff, office staff, and production staff communicate to get project information to one central information source?

Reviewing The Plans

You have to schedule time to review the plans with the architect. If you find anything in error, or not clear, ask for clarification immediately. Your reputation, quality of work, bid price, and ultimately profits, depend on clarity and understanding of the total project.

Tip
The best time for a plan review with an architect is before the estimating or bid process starts.

Inspections by the Architect or Designer

You have to schedule inspections by the architect or designer when the contract requires it. Normally these inspections are similar to the inspection requirements for the local building department. Examples are:

- Before pouring concrete
- Before backfilling over drainlines
- After framing is complete
- When the electrical system is finished
- After plumbing rough in
- Other technical or custom operations

"If at first you don't succeed, you're running about average."
M. H. Anderson

Sometimes you may only have to schedule architectural inspections before any progress payments are made by the owner or lending institution. Establish a clear understanding of what is expected by the architect or designer with regard to inspections and consultations.

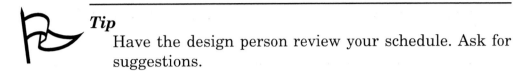

Tip
Have the design person review your schedule. Ask for suggestions.

Suppliers

After your schedule is formalized, it is time to talk to suppliers about materials. Some things to consider when talking to suppliers are:

- Price
- Payment terms
- Return policy
- Delivery policy and cost
- Promises of cooperation
- Selection, and more

You want to be sure that your supplier will deliver:

- To the correct project
- In the correct order
- In the correct amounts
- At the correct time

A project always includes people who have a role in supporting the project, but are not under your direct control as employees. Management is getting them to do their required pieces of the project correctly and on time.

Encourage the owner to select any items they are to choose for the project as early as possible. Not only do these selections have to be made, but there will often be backorders and other delays.

Suppliers And Service

Since raw building materials are generally a commodity (the same quality product), service is usually the only important factor when choosing a supplier. Choosing the correct supplier can make your project easy instead of difficult.

Tip

Many suppliers offer discounts of one or two percent if payment is made quickly, within 10 days for example. A typical supplier invoice may state "2/10, net 30." This means you get a two percent discount if paid within 10 days, otherwise, payment is due in 30 days. Take advantage of this if possible.

"You grow up the day you have the first real laugh at yourself."
Ethel Barrymore

"Just in Time" (JIT) Deliveries

Just in time delivery is a simple concept that goes a long way toward keeping inventory costs down. The main concept behind JIT deliveries is, even though you may have ordered materials in advance, you do not have them delivered until they are needed. This way your responsibility for the materials on the project site is kept to a minimum.

Most suppliers that make deliveries are used to operating this way. They will gladly coordinate delivery of material in stages, depending on the size of the project. For example, loads may be divided in the following manner:

- Posts and beams, and T&G decking first
- Wall framing material and ceiling joists next
- Roof framing material and sheathing next
- Special order items like laminated beams or trusses may comprise separate loads
- The next load could include such items as:

  - Exterior doors and windows
  - Exterior trim and siding

- Hardwood flooring and underlay materials can come next
- Other interior items such as:

  - Interior doors
  - Interior trim
  - Cabinets

Warning
Suppliers may charge an additional delivery fee for small loads. However, the added convenience and reduced risk of theft and/or vandalism may be worth the additional cost.

JIT delivery often saves money by:

- Reducing on-the-project material handling
- Preventing work slowdown because materials are in the way
- Reducing risk of injury due to a cluttered project site

Inspectors

Inspectors from various agencies will visit (invited and uninvited) your project site. You need to schedule inspections by:

- Building inspectors from the local government agency in charge of building in that area
- The owner or architect under terms of the contract
- A loan officer from your construction project lending institution, if required by them

Your prime concern as general contractor is to:

- Make sure work to be inspected is complete and ready for inspection.
- See that a required inspection occurs before work starts on any subsequent part of the project.

"Some people approach every problem with an open mouth."
Adalai Stevenson

Warning
Government building inspectors have the authority to have you undo any work that has covered another phase of the project for which a required inspection was omitted. For example:

- Flooring that covers insulation
- Concrete that covers rough plumbing or electrical wiring that required inspection

You will not be able to proceed until the building inspector officially inspects certain parts of the project and has signed the appropriate line on the project inspection record.

Improper scheduling of inspections causes sudden delays. Sudden delays could result in other additional expenses in the form of:

- Time spent rectifying the problem to the satisfaction of the inspector
- Money spent to pay subcontractors who will charge you for their time spent waiting
- Rescheduling other phases of the project
- Rescheduling other pending projects

"Who begins too much accomplishes little."
German proverb

Inspections Take Time

Project inspections require that some time be set aside.

Tip
We suggest that inspections of these kinds be included in your written or diagramed schedule (see Exhibit 5, "Critical Path Method" at the end of Chapter 3: "Scheduling Systems") like any other phase of the project.

You should determine whose schedule will have to be the most flexible: yours or the inspector's. Owners, architects and even bank officers are often flexible enough to accommodate the project. A one-day notice may be sufficient.

It is best to keep communication open with a steady flow of progress reports. Give these inspectors as much advance notice as possible.

Note
Typically a delayed inspection by a loan officer will not directly delay a project, but it may directly delay the disbursement of funds. It may then be a short matter of time before the project shuts down.

Dealing With Local Government Building Agencies

Building inspectors may require additional consideration. Most building agencies attempt to accommodate contractors, providing you follow their procedures. In order to get a same day or a next day inspection, the agency will often require that requests be called in by a certain time.

This does not always guarantee an inspection will happen when the recorded message says it will. Inspection agencies work on a first-come-first-served basis. In some localities, agencies are understaffed and inspectors are unable to get to every project on a given day. As pointed out, this one-day delay can have expensive consequences.

Tip

Sometimes a prompt inspection is more critical than other times. For instance, a request for a morning inspection of form work for a foundation can be especially critical if you have the concrete trucks scheduled for 1 p.m. the same day.

In such cases, be sure to communicate directly with the inspector. Most agencies have specific times of the day when inspectors are at the agency to handle such calls. Inspectors will often give such inspections priority.

Get to know the inspection agency with jurisdiction over your project. Find out if you are dealing with a city, county, or contracted agency. Ask other contractors in the area about the reliability of the agency involved.

Try to build flexibility into your schedule by having other phases of the project ready to be worked on while waiting for an inspection.

Nothing is impossible for someone who doesn't have to do it themselves.

Inspection "Psychology"

Depending on the type of inspection, and your experience with them, an official building inspection can involve various degrees of stress. Because of the evolving nature of building codes, even the most experienced contractor can mistakenly violate some code requirements.

It is important to remain calm when the inspector confronts you with such an issue. You will find that receiving an *inspection memo* from a building official is much like receiving a traffic ticket from a police officer because your car is in violation of some standard. Sometimes the best you can do is to politely accept the slip and go about fixing the problem.

Options

What the on-site building inspector decrees is not always the last word. You have a number of options. You could:

■ Discuss the issue with the plans checker (code analyst) who originally reviewed the plans.

Sometimes the problem revolves around an issue of material substitution. On-site inspectors are not usually permitted to accept deviations from the approved plans. The plans checker may find the substitute material acceptable and would be willing to resolve the issue quietly with the on-site inspector.

■ Other options include:

◆ Filing an "Alternate Materials and Method Application" or, if your request is denied
◆ Filing an appeal to the Hearings Board

> **Note**
> Under no circumstances will any of the above inspectors be willing to ignore the building code. However, certain groups of building code officials who review code challenges have the authority to exercise a broader interpretation of the code. Variances are permitted regarding the letter of the code as long as the intent of the code is not violated.

This appeals process can take weeks to complete. Fees have to be paid for some steps in the appeals process and tend to increase in cost the further you proceed.

Uninvited Inspections

While the previous inspections are planned into your schedule, there are some inspections that can happen without notice. Surprise inspections can come from:

Bove's Theory: "The remaining work to finish in order to reach your goal increases as the deadline approaches."

- Occupational Safety and Health Administration (OSHA)
- The enforcement division of the state licensing or registration agency
- Other building code officials

Your best safeguard for these inspections is knowledge.

As with all inspection processes, the best policy is to remain calm. If problems arise, ask that the problem be clearly defined. Determine if the easiest solution is simply to correct the problem or to formally appeal.

People and Contracting

The amount of interaction with people increases as the contractor's business grows. You may find yourself spending less time building and more time administrating. Dealing with people related to the project is just as important as the actual construction.

Summary

This chapter dealt with issues about the people connected to the project. Those you typically find involved with a project are:

I understand fully, therefore I can act correctly.

- Owners
- Employees
- Subcontractors
- Architects, designers, and engineers
- Suppliers
- Inspectors

Every aspect of scheduling involves a person who is to do something connected with your project. Practice proper "people skills" to help your project go smoothly. Promptly communicate every item affecting the project to the correct person.

Chapter 3

Scheduling Systems

This chapter covers these specific scheduling systems:

- Critical Path Method (CPM)
- Bar Chart scheduling
- Calendar scheduling

Project "Breakdown"

Planning comes ahead of scheduling. You plan how you will deal with the project details, then build the schedule with all detail items included.

All systems of scheduling begin by breaking down the project into its parts. This process begins with estimating. As explained in Chapter 1: "General Scheduling," the "Estimate Sheet" is the tool for this. However, estimating does not cover everything necessary to put together a complete schedule. Other important factors to consider are:

- Time between projects
- Waiting for permits to be issued
- Curing and/or drying time for concrete, paint, plaster and so forth
- Delivery times for critical items and other materials
- Inspections

Project Breakdown Checklist

A project breakdown checklist consists of the parts of the project that you are scheduling.

The estimate sheet, plans and specifications, and the project contract are useful tools for developing a project breakdown checklist. (See these headings in Chapter 1:"General Scheduling.")

First, identify each major phase or activity of the project. For example:

- Permit process (if you are responsible)
- Pre-project meetings

- Critical items that need to be ordered
- Site preparation
- Excavation
- Foundation
- Framing, etc.

Next, break down each major activity as much as necessary to clearly define what is required to finish the project. For example:

- Site preparation

  - Delivery of dumpster and other project start-up supplies (portable "rest room," etc.)
  - Layout (transit work, batter boards, stakes and string)

- Excavation

  - Clearing
  - Footings
  - Backfilling
  - Finish grading, etc.

- Foundation

  - Form work

    - Footings
    - Stem wall
    - Block work
    - Steel (rebar) work, etc.

  - Pour concrete
  - Cure time, etc.

- Framing

  - Mudsills
  - Posts and beams
  - Decking
  - Walls, etc.

The schedule of a project is the process indicating when each element of the operation starts and finishes.

The plans or working drawings of a project are like a "chart" for a jazz musician; the basics are covered, but most of the finer details are not noted. A carpenter, like the jazz musician, takes the drawings and, with personal expertise and direction from the specifications, will make a complete building. As with jazz, there are a number of players: Carpenter, Designer, Inspector, Owner and Contractor.

The Smaller the Better

Break the project down into as many parts as are useful. Your breakdown checklist is the best place for detail. Scheduling is like the costing process; an item completely forgotten does the most harm.

When using a formal scheduling system, such as a calendar schedule or CPM diagram, you probably will not use all of the activities you listed on your breakdown checklist.

Too much detail on your calendar or diagram tends to create visual clutter. However, your checklist provides the means to ensure that each major category on your calendar or CPM diagram includes important smaller activities.

Activity Duration

The next step in developing any scheduling system is to determine how long each task will take.

This depends not only on the work, but on other criteria. You will need to consider the:

Activities such as ordering materials and notifiying sub-contractors belong on the schedule.

- Number of workers performing each activity
- Skill level of the workers as compared to the com-plexity of the activity
- Working conditions such as weather, terrain, and or site accessibility
- Budget restraints
- Other scheduling factors that would speed up or slow down the work activity

You will also have to consider the duration of subcontract work. As stated in Chapter 2: "Dealing with Others on the Job," procedures such as pre-project meetings and preliminary scheduling will greatly benefit accuracy.

However, as any contractor who has been in business for awhile will testify, construction projects are notorious for taking longer than anticipated. This is true whether the project is an apartment complex or a bathroom remodel. (See "Laws of Nature," in Chapter 2: "Dealing with Others on the Job.")

Scheduling Benefits

Because of the variable nature of most construction projects (especially remodeling projects), the need to develop a written or diagrammed schedule becomes important.

Developing a project schedule does not guarantee you will complete the project on time, but it does provide a way to see how close you are to your time estimate and to make the necessary adjustments. Knowing when to make these adjustments is the main benefit of project scheduling.

Evaluation

Besides keeping track of a project to complete it on time, scheduling systems also provide a controlled means of evaluating the project for:

Listen with the same intensity and concern you use when you talk.

- Present project cost effectiveness
- Future project cost estimating and scheduling

Scheduling is like any other part of the contracting business. The better organized and developed your systems of operation are, the more capable you will be in evaluating present business procedures. You will then be able to make helpful adjustments to your scheduling for future projects.

For many contractors who operate on a relatively small scale, especially those in the remodeling business, there is a tendency to believe that estimating methods of any kind are more trouble than they are worth.

The claim is that projects are diverse, that is, what is true for one job will not always be true for the next. The point is that by establishing a method for scheduling projects, you establish a written history that you can use to compensate for such diversity.

Methods of Estimating Activity Time

We will examine two methods of estimating the duration of work activities on a project.

The first method is simply based on previous experience.

Warning

Previous experience does not mean, "Well, let's see, how long did that task take Pete the last time. I think it was a day and a half. Or was it two days?"

Previous Experience

Previous experience has to be recorded to become a method of estimating. This record will note specific results with information on:

- What exactly was done
- Who did the work
- Comments regarding the time spent to complete the activity

Averaged Time

This second method also uses previous experience. However, an averaged time is also used.

Change orders can directly affect the schedule. Without exception, they have to be in writing. New materials or extra work have to be worked in. Agreement has to be on money and time.

Average the time based on three different time estimates for each work activity. Try this procedure to determine your three estimates:

- Estimate the average time needed to complete the activity under normal conditions. Call this estimate "Ta" for the Time-average estimate.
- Make another estimate where everything that can go wrong will go wrong. Call this estimate "Tp" for the Time-pessimistic estimate. (Also known as the "Murphy Estimate")
- Base a third estimate on the optimistic view that everything will go perfectly. Call this estimate "To" for Time-optimistic estimate.

Use the following formula to find the "Te," or Time-expected estimate:

$$Te = \frac{To + 4Ta + Tp}{6}$$

For example, if the average time (Ta) is five (5) days, the best possible time (To) might be three (3) days. If everything falls apart, the worst possible time (Tp), could take nine days. The formula would look like this:

$$Te = \frac{3 + (4 \times 5) + 9}{6}$$

$$Te = \frac{3 + 20 + 9}{6} = 5.3$$

As you can see, the estimate would be 5.3 days.

Tip

This formula is ideal for bidding purposes because it places an emphasis on the average time to complete a construction project activity (Ta is multiplied by 4), while also factoring in the worst and best case possibilities.

Whether you use a single estimate or some kind of averaging method for estimating project activity duration, experience is always the best gauge. The accuracy of your experience gauge is enhanced by developing a good scheduling system.

Benefit From Past Successes

Keeping records of similar completed jobs will give information on:

- The correct steps for producing a basic part of a project
- Timing the delivery of materials to be available when needed, but not before they will be needed
- Any circumstances that can affect project completion time

One of the greatest pleasures in life is doing what people say you can't do.

Give Scheduling a Chance

As stated, this chapter explores three scheduling systems:

- Critical Path Method (CPM)
- Bar Chart scheduling
- Calendar scheduling

Depending on the scale of your projects, some of the procedures in these systems may seem too complex or time consuming to be of use. However, this won't be the case once you practice using these systems. In fact, these systems can help create profitable business habits. You may find yourself wondering how you ever handled a project without them.

Warning: Dates on calanders are closer than they appear.

Note

Keep in mind that even if you do not use one of the following scheduling systems, eventually you will be associated with a project that does.

By learning the basics of these systems now, you will be better prepared to work with them when you encounter them in the future.

Keep It Simple

In order to facilitate explaining the different systems, we will use a relatively simple project .

On the following page, you will find a "Project Breakdown and Duration Checklist" for a 1-room addition (without plumbing). Assume that it is a family room addition or a master bedroom.

Also, the estimated duration time for each general activity should not be a guideline for estimating any similar projects of your own.

Note

As you can see, the "activity" list on our breakdown checklist is not very detailed. However, even for a simple job like this, a more detailed checklist would be best.

As stated in the beginning of this chapter, you would not need to put all the details on your CPM diagram, chart, or calendar. However, such details ensure more complete scheduling of your project.

If the schedule process for our 1-room addition began and ended with the activity checklist, you might think the project would last about 37 work days. By using specific scheduling systems let's see how we can improve on this.

Critical Path Method

The Critical Path Method is a production control system that evolved from procedures developed during WWII. Entire books have been written about reading and developing a CPM diagram for the most complex jobs, like building the Hoover Dam.

The Critical Path Method (CPM) is a planning and scheduling system that uses arrows, circles, and numbers to create a diagram. The diagram illustrates the sequence of all work activity involved in a construction project.

> ### Note
> CPM diagrams can become so complex that they resemble a circuit plan for AT&T. However, once you are able to recognize the basic principles of the Critical Path Method, and once you have taken the time to experiment with the diagramming process, you will see its usefulness for construction scheduling.

The greatest value of the Critical Path Method is that it identifies the "critical path" through the job.

Finding the Critical Path

The critical path through a project is that path which includes every critical part of the project. On a CPM diagram, the longest path (in terms of adding up the time each critical part of the project takes along the different routes of the diagram) equals the least possible time to complete the entire project.

By comparison, the least flexible path would include every part of the project, critical or not, and would be seen to delay the project.

The Longest Path

To understand the concept of the longest path through a project, let's look at a simple project.

In this example, we are burying a water line from a well to a house. While one worker is putting the plastic pipe together, the other worker is digging the trench.

It takes only three (3) hours to put the pipe together, but it takes

Owners don't remember that their project was started promptly. They do, however, remember when delays occur and how you react when the project seems to be out of control.

Exhibit 4: Project Breakdown and Duration Checklist

Project Breakdown and Duration Checklist

Activity	Duration (Working Days)
Site Preparation and Layout	1.00
Excavation	1.00
Form work	1.50
Pour concrete	.50
Cure concrete	1.00
Remove forms	.75
Drain pipes	.75
Backfill	.25
Prepare crawl space	.25
Posts and beams	.50
Insulation	.75
Decking	1.00
Wall framing	2.00
Roof framing	2.00
Roofing	2.00
Gutters	.50
Doors and windows	.50
Electrical	1.50
Siding and exterior trim	3.00
Plaster work	3.00
Painting	5.50
Finish carpentry	3.00
Carpet	.50
Finish grading	.50
Landscaping	2.00
Sanitation	1.25
Total duration in working days:	36.50

two (2) days to dig the trench. Putting this project in diagram form, let's identify the longest ("critical") path:

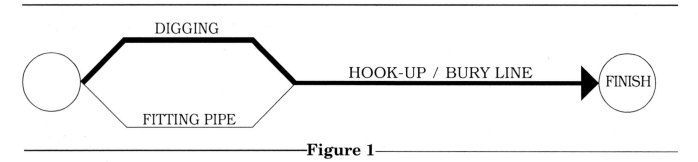

DIGGING

HOOK-UP / BURY LINE FINISH

FITTING PIPE

—————**Figure 1**—————

As you can see, the longest path through the job is the one that includes the trench digging. This is the critical path, because it includes all the tasks to be done to complete the project.

This same path takes the least amount of time to complete the project. The project has to take at least two (2) days plus the time needed for hook-up and burying the line.

Tip

The above concept is perhaps the most confusing aspect of the critical path system of scheduling.

It is important that you have a clear understanding of how the "critical path" is both the longest path through the project while also being the fastest overall time in which the project can be completed.

Look at Figure 1 again. Get a good grasp of this concept before continuing.

Float Time

Float time is spare time. Using our water-line job as an example, you can see that the worker putting the pipe together has a lot more float time than the worker digging the trench. If the worker putting the pipe together takes several hours longer than expected, the completion of the project will not be delayed. However, if digging the trench takes longer, then the entire project will take longer.

The Critical Path Method is a visual aid for identifying where and when float time is available. Properly used, the contractor can take advantage of the spare time available from some parts of the project to facilitate work on other parts.

Using the example in Figure 1, the contractor would be able to adjust the schedule for this project. The contractor could arrange the schedule so that the worker fitting the pipe could also help dig the trench. The contractor could schedule this to happen before or after the pipe fitting is complete. The pipe fitting activity, which is not along the critical path, is flexible.

By adjusting the schedule in this way, the overall time for the project is reduced. The most efficient use of labor is attained. There are many possibilities for managing float time. However, these possibilities become limited unless you have a scheduling system that identifies if, where, and when float time is available.

Two Part System

The CPM system is actually a two part system. It is a planning system, and a scheduling system.

CPM Planning

As with all scheduling and estimating systems, planning is accomplished through the CPM by:

- Identifying each major phase of the project
- Breaking down each major phase as much as necessary to clearly define stages of work activities
- Making certain that each construction activity identified is in its proper dependent position (proper sequence)

You can do this by always asking the same question for each activity: "What has to be completed first before this part of the project can begin."

Note

The CPM diagram does not show what date a work activity will begin or end. The diagram simply shows the sequence of work activity. For example, before you can pour the concrete you must first build the form.

The tail (left side of the arrow-line) represents the beginning of a construction activity. The tip (right side of the arrow-line) represents the end of an activity.

Circles are used as markers between each specific work activity. Each circle represents the end of one construction activity and the beginning of another.

This point (when one activity ends and another begins) is called an event. (Figure 2 illustrates this).

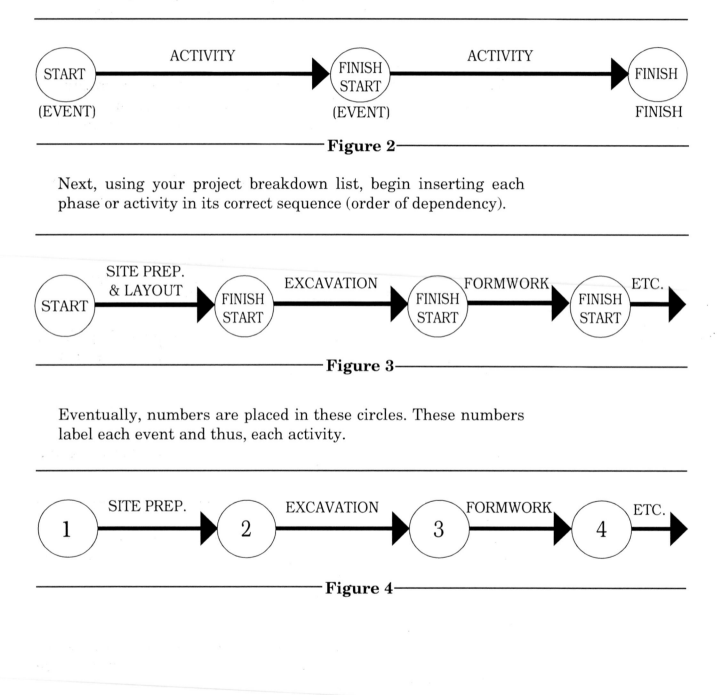

Figure 2

Next, using your project breakdown list, begin inserting each phase or activity in its correct sequence (order of dependency).

Figure 3

Eventually, numbers are placed in these circles. These numbers label each event and thus, each activity.

Figure 4

Tip
Think of the numbers within the circles as event names.

- Site preparation and layout is activity 1-2;
- Excavation is activity 2-3;
- Formwork is activity 3-4, etc.

Rule of Dependency

The rule of dependency states that lower numbered activities have to be completed before higher numbered activities can begin. Thus, the event number at the tail of an arrow is always lower than the event number at the tip.

When doing your own critical path diagram for a project, do not number the events until you have carefully checked the entire diagram to determine that:

"It's a funny thing about life; if you refuse to accept anything but the best, you very often get it."
Somerset Maugham

- All phases of the project have been included
- All phases are in the correct dependent sequence
- The critical path has been identified

We inserted event numbers early in the procedure to simplify the teaching process. It is easier to refer to something that has a name, for example, "event 6" or "activity 6-7."

The problem with inserting event numbers prematurely is that if one activity is out of sequence and needs to be moved, it affects every event number that follows. This can add up to a lot of erasing if you insert numbers early.

Note
This numerical naming of events in not as crucial on small jobs as on large projects that require higher levels of sophistication.

Branching Out

Most projects will have activities that do not depend on each other, but they can start at the same point in the schedule. This is where a CPM diagram branches out.

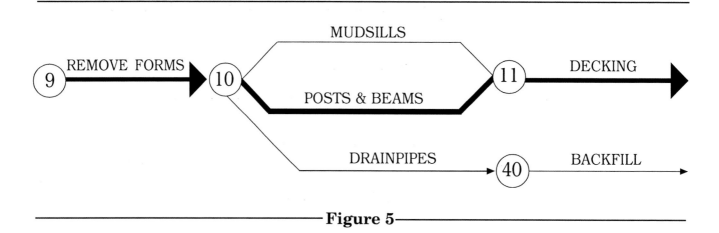

Figure 5

Notice the gap between event numbers shown in Figure 5. "Drainpipes" begins with event 10 and ends with event 40.

When numbering events, you will always give priority to activities along the critical path. However, each time a branch rejoins the critical path, all the activities leading up to that event have to be completed first.

This numbering system follows this order of priority by sometimes zig-zagging around the diagram. In Figure 5, "Drainpipes" is not on the critical path, and there is no need to complete it until event 40 is done.

> "Do not put off until tomorrow what can be enjoyed today."
> Josh Billings

Tip

You will better understand this by looking at the complete CPM diagram for the one room addition (Exhibit 5) at the end of this chapter. Look at the end of the project, events 39 to 46. Notice that events 40 through 45, which are drawn near the beginning of the diagram, need to be completed before event 46 can begin.

Remember, one branch will rejoin another branch at that point in the project where the activities along that path have to be completed before another part of the project can begin. This follows the rule of dependency.

"Dummy" Lines

"Dummy" lines are simply dotted lines used in the branching out process of a CPM diagram. "Dummy" lines tend to complicate drawing the work flow of a project. However, on a sophisticated level, the use of dotted (dummy) lines serves two functions:

- Identifying different activities with different event numbers
- Indicating no time lapse between the event numbers connected by the dotted line

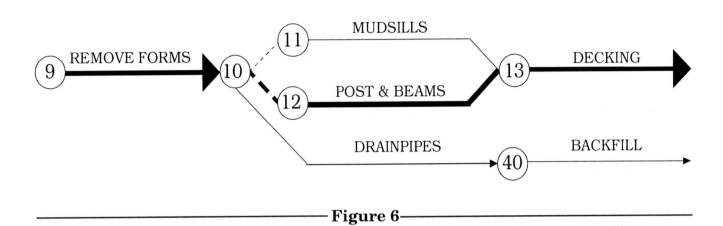

Figure 6

Identification Purposes

Activities happening in the same stage need different identification numbers. Dotted lines (known as dummy lines) separate activities that can happen at the same time, but which need a different event number for identification.

Look at Figure 5 and notice that both "Mudsills" and "Posts and beams" have the same number identification, 10-11. On a large project, this could cause communication problems. For this reason dummy lines are used and artificial event numbers are added.

A dummy line creates artificial events 11 and 12. A dummy line gives the two activities different identification numbers:

- "Mudsills" equals Activity 11-13
- "Posts and beams" equals Activity 12-13

"A problem is a chance to do your best."
Duke Ellington

In this case, "Mudsills" and "Posts and beams" occur after event 10 and both have to be complete before event 13 can begin.

Zero Time Duration

There is no duration associated with dummy lines. This becomes more important for clarity as a CPM diagram develops multiple branches. An activity along one branch may depend on an activity on another branch.

Activity 10-40, "Drainpipes," has a duration associated with it. A dummy line is not used here. However, "Drainpipes" also depends on form work being removed.

Keep the process simple by always keeping the basic process in mind:

- Place events in the correct sequence
- When inserting an activity, find the earliest place (on the diagram) it can happen. All other activities that have to first be completed will have arrows leading up to and connecting with that activity
- Branch activities do not have to rejoin any other lines unless a new part of the project depends on that line of activities
- Do not worry about dummy lines, but do understand what they indicate. Use them when the need becomes apparent

CPM Scheduling

The scheduling aspect of the Critical Path Method identifies the duration of each activity and a working timetable for the entire project.

The numbers designating "duration" and "timetable" will be added directly on the CPM diagram.

"Many of life's failures are people who did not know how close they were to success when they gave up."
Thomas Edison

Duration

The number of work days needed to complete each activity is written under that activity. Partial days are expressed in decimals (.5 for ½ day).

The length of an activity line does not equal its duration. The duration (number of work days) is designated by the number below each activity line. (See Figure 7.)

Note
The length of an activity arrow typically has nothing to do with how long a work activity is expected to take. Activities appearing one above the other will not necessarily be happening at the same time.

However, some contractors have developed hybrid CPM/calendar systems that are laid out on a calendar gridwork where the CPM diagram is then drawn to a time scale.

Project Timetables

Each event (the ending of one activity and the beginning of another) is predicted to occur at a particular phase of the project, not always a particular date or time.

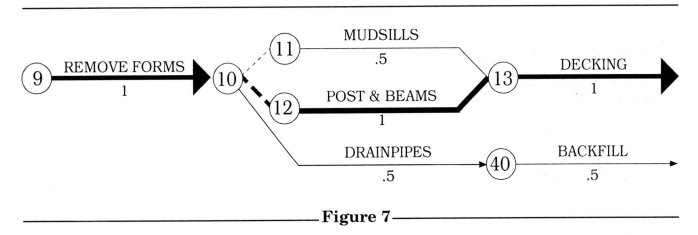

─── **Figure 7** ───

Earliest Event Times

To determine how many workdays are necessary to reach a particular event, simply add the duration times (the numbers you have placed under each activity) of all preceding work activities. That is the earliest an event can happen. (Weekends and holidays are not considered in CPM diagrams.)

Warning
Always follow the longest time path to each event.

The sum of activity durations leading up to an event is placed in a rectangle over the event on the arrow diagram. Figure 8 illustrates this beginning with event 9. Let's assume that event 9 begins five working days from the beginning of the project.

In Figure 8, you can see that activity 9-10 (Removing forms) has a duration of one day. This duration has been added to a total previous duration of five (5) days. Thus, the earliest event 10 can begin is six (6) working days into the project.

The earliest time in working days event 40 can begin is in 6½ working days.

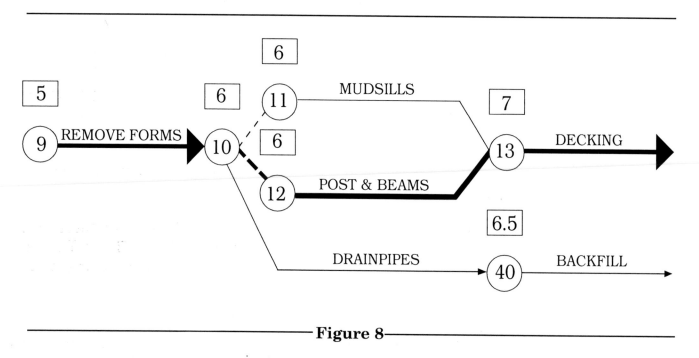

Figure 8

Event 13 has two paths leading to it. One through activity 11-13 (Mudsills); the other through activity 12-13 (Posts and Beams). Following the rule of selecting the longest path, the earliest event time for event 13 would be 7 days as opposed to 6½ days. Therefore, the critical path travels through event 12-13.

Work this process until each event has an earliest event time written in a rectangular box next to it.

Latest Event Times

You should next determine the latest event times for each event. Typically, these times (number of working days) are placed in triangles ($\triangledown$) next to each event.

Every activity phase of a project leads to another activity phase. The latest event time represents the maximum number of days into

Records kept at the project site are most accurate for later project analysis. Don't rely on memories.

the project in which a particular phase has to be completed to keep the project on time.

To calculate the number of workdays for the latest event time, begin at the completion of the project and work back. The last rectangular box (earliest event time) is where you start.

Subtract the duration of the activity preceding each event to get the latest event time for the preceding event. These numbers are typically in triangles next to the earliest event times within the rectangles. (See Figure 9 page 70.)

You will find that as you proceed along the critical path, each earliest event time equals each latest event time. When the earliest and latest event times are the same, this indicates that you are on the critical path and that the activity leading up to such an event has no float time.

If any one of these events on the critical path is delayed, the entire project will also be delayed.

For those activities and events off the critical path there is a difference between the earliest and latest times. This difference represents the float time available for each activity leading to the event off the critical path.

Using Figure 9, assume that "Decking" lies on the critical path. Working back, notice that the earliest and latest event times are the same for event 12, that is on the critical path. Notice that event 11, which is not on the critical path, has a ½-day (.5) of float time.

This is like the original mini-project in Figure 1, where the worker digging the trench had no time to spare, while the worker fitting the pipe had plenty of spare time.

This process works only if you abide by the CPM rule of always following the longest path when calculating earliest event times.

Quality work and working conditions are the goal of all project managers. Improving site conditions and worker output should not be an exercise in spotting errors. Rather, what is being done well.

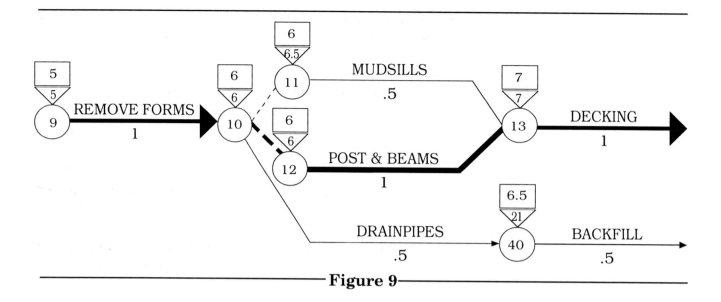

Figure 9

CPM Total Time

The sum of the durations of all activities lying along the critical path is the total duration in workdays for the project. Exhibit 5 at the end of this chapter illustrates how our one room addition project would look on a CPM diagram schedule. Practicing what we just learned, you should now be able to read this diagram.

The critical path is highlighted by the thicker line. It is the path that follows the longest route in activity durations through the project. Notice how earliest event times (the numbers in the rectangles) match the latest event times (the numbers in the triangles) along the critical path.

The total time needed for the project equals the total duration of this path. For our 1-room addition, the critical path has a total of 28.25 workdays. Compare this total with the total of 36.5 workdays indicated on our project's Activity Breakdown and Duration Checklist.

If the project calls for 12 subcontractors during the course of construction and each one completes their work within 2 days of the scheduled start and finish time, this could add 24 days to the project. This is true, without taking into account the weather. Doing the work within 2 days is not bad service, it is about average.

Remodel contracting can be compared to fighting a war with a rented army. Your contractor or you, if you choose to manage your project, cannot order a trade subcontractor to be on the site on a certain day and time. You go with the flow and try to keep the project going.

By using the Critical Path Method of scheduling, our perspective of the room addition project has been greatly enhanced. We now know:

"There is the greatest practical benefit in making a few failures early in life."
T. H. Huxley

- A more accurate total duration for the project
- Which activities are "critical" (meaning that a delay with any one or more of these activities will delay the entire project)
- Where and how much float time is available for those noncritical activities. (The difference between earliest and latest event times is the amount of float time available.)
- The correct sequence of project events in terms of the dependency between all construction activities

Should You Use CPM

There are many books about CPM scheduling. Some authors claim that designing a CPM diagram for our 1-room addition would be a waste of time and money. This may be true if the CPM diagram is too detailed. This happens when too many activities are listed.

However, by keeping the breakdown categories in the diagram at a reasonable amount for the project, you can reduce the complexity of your diagram.

Experiment with CPM scheduling on your next project. You may find the most difficult part is finding a long enough piece of paper to draw on.

We suggest strips of drafting paper or simply taping regular 8.5 X 11 typing or graph paper together. Just add sheets of paper as the diagram grows.

We have also found that CPM diagramming is helpful when you formulate a project chart or calendar schedule.

Delays

If any activity along the critical path takes longer than the estimated duration, this affects the entire project in terms of:

- Earliest event times
- Latest event times
- Total time for the project

Note
There is also the possibility that a delay could cause the critical path to change. For example, if an event off of the critical path does not start before the latest event time for that activity, then this branch could become the longer (critical) path through the project.

"Common sense is not so common." Voltaire

Bar Chart Scheduling

Exhibit 6, "Bar Chart Schedule," shows another system for scheduling our one room addition. (The example uses X's, you may use solid lines or bars as well.)

Although this method does not accomplish as much as a CPM diagram or a calendar schedule, it is an easy way to gain perspective on the project schedule. It also helps you see the relationships between various work activities.

Creating a bar chart is similar to any other scheduling system. The project, of course, is broken down into its parts. For simplicity, the duration of each activity is expressed in full days.

Bar charts are used for larger, longer term projects, where half days are less important. However, feel free to indicate half days on your charts if you find it beneficial.

First Things First

As you think about project activities, you see certain categories that occur in distinct stages at different times during the project. List these activities in the order they take place.

For example, insulation for our 1-room addition happens initially in the subfloor structure, after the walls, roof and roofing have been completed. Electrical work also has distinct rough and finish phases. Painting also occurs in stages.

These categories (insulation, electrical, and painting) are listed where they begin.

This is done to assist in identifying what work activities depend on other work activities.

Remember, one of the primary goals of any scheduling system is to show the dependency between parts of the project. A chart offers an easy way to see such dependencies.

Keeping Good Notes

Place notes on your charts for special stages in the project. For example, note what construction activities require an inspection before the next activity can start. (See Exhibit 6.)

Calendar Scheduling

Calendar scheduling is a bar chart on a calendar. Exhibit 7 shows this scheduling system for our one room addition. (We have omitted weekends.)

Advantages

The primary advantage of calendar scheduling is that it pinpoints construction activities to specific dates. Another advantage is that it is ideal for small projects. It is also useful for coordinating subcontractor and supplier schedules for:

- Start and finish dates for other projects
- Delivery dates for supplies and materials
- Scheduling disbursement of progress payments
- Working around vacations and holidays

"It is common sense to take a method and try it. If it fails, admit it frankly and try another. But above all, try something."
Franklin D. Roosevelt

Disadvantages

The primary disadvantage of calendar scheduling is that the critical path is not obvious. It is not easy to see critical activities and float time. On a small project, the experienced contractor can overcome this.

Which is the Best Scheduling System?

Your best scheduling system is the one you can use successfully. Any system is better than none. By experimenting with different systems, you learn to develop a method that works best for a project.

If it works best for the project, it is best for your business.

Scheduling Software

Many computer programs help design construction schedules. Most of these programs automate the scheduling you have read about.

You will benefit most from these programs if:

■ You are already comfortable using a computer.
■ You have a clear understanding of what your construction scheduling needs are.
■ You can match your existing scheduling process to the computer program.

"Do what you can, with what you have, with what you are."
Theodore Roosevelt

Scheduling on Computers

No computer scheduling program will complete your construction schedules for you. You must first know how to break down a project into its parts. Then you can enter that information into the computer.

Computer programs generally work well for those who take the time to learn how to use them. Computers are a tool like any other. They will allow you to use skills more accurately and faster. Schedule changes, in particular, can often be handled more efficiently with a computer. Printouts of these changes are more readily available for distribution to subcontractors and others who need updates.

Tip

Measure the time, money, and effort spent setting up a computer scheduling system against how much you will benefit from using such a system.

A computer will always show you the shortest time periods for a task. Therefore, you have a schedule that is likely to be tight because it relies on all going well. You have to look closely to adjust for potential problems. Be very careful with making committments!

Final Hints and Tips

The goal of project management and scheduling is to get everything done on time and according to your promises, while still having a life.

You can effectively use many variations and combinations of these three scheduling systems. There are no set rules. Experiment and use what is best for your operation.

The techniques discussed in this chapter are designed to introduce scheduling and supply some tools to help you get started.

Experience and common sense weigh heavily in setting up schedules and will compliment any method or combination of methods. Always add extra time as a fudge factor. Jobs rarely run as smoothly in real life as they do on paper.

Summary

Your scheduling system is the process that will get your projects completed in the most efficient manner. Each system has to begin with a breakdown of the tasks to be done in the project. This chapter covered:

- Important Critical Path Methods
- Bar Chart Scheduling
- Calendar Scheduling

Use the information in this chapter to build the most useful scheduling system for your contracting specialty.

Exhibit 5: Critical Path Method Diagram (left half)

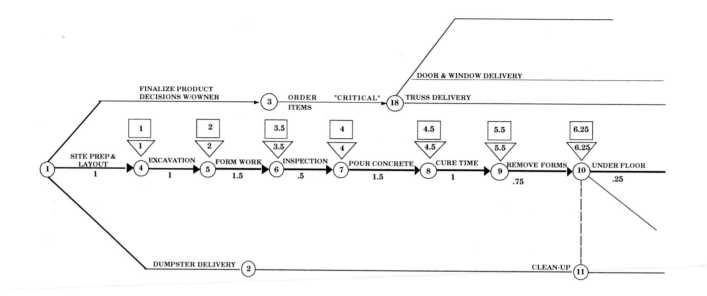

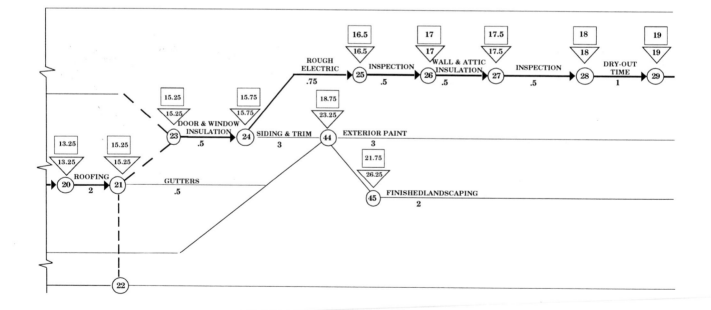

Exhibit 5: Critical Path Method Diagram (right half)

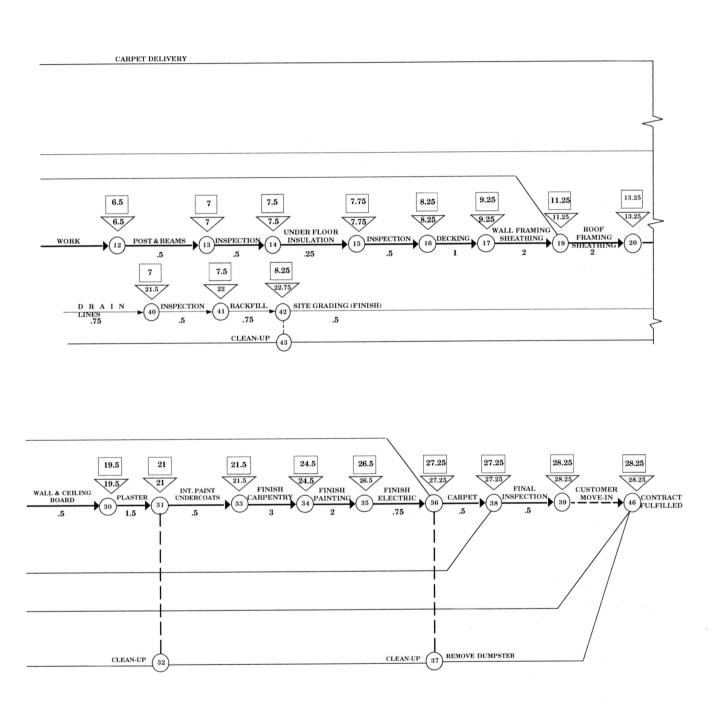

Exhibit 6: Sample of Bar Chart Schedule

| Project SMITH JOB
Address: 321 W. 6TH | | | | | | | | Start Date: 3/1 | | | |

Project Activity: Work Day #	1	2	3	4	5	6	7	8	9	10
ORDER CRITICAL ITEMS	X									
SITE PREP & LAYOUT	X									
EXCAVATION		X								
FORMWORK			X	X✓						
POUR CONCRETE					⊗					
CURE CONCRETE						X				
REMOVE FORMSS							X			
DRAINPIPES							X✓			
* BACKFILL								X		
UNDER FLOOR WORK								X✓		
POSTS & BEAMS									X✓	
* INSULATION										X✓
DECKING										
WALL FRAMING										
ROOF FRAMING										
* ROOFING										
* GUTTERS										
DOORS & WINDOWS										
* ELECTRICAL										
SIDING & EXT. TRIM										
PLASTER WORK										
PAINTING										
FINISH CARPENTRY										
* CARPETING										
* FINISH GRADING										
* LANDSCAPING										
SANITATION (DUMPSTER - CLEAN-UP)	X							X		

✓ INDICATES INSPECTION REQUIRED

⊗ IF POSSIBLE, SCHEDULE FOR A FRIDAY - REDUCE PROJECT DURATION BY 1 DAY (IF CURE TIME ON A WEEKEND)

* INDICATES SUBCONTRACT WORK

Exhibit 6: Sample of Bar Chart Schedule, continued

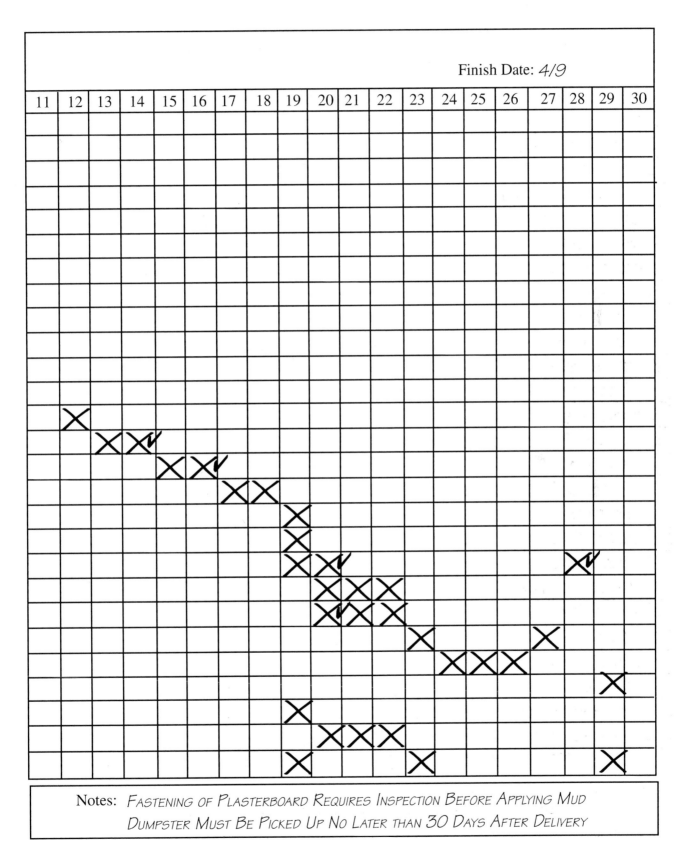

Finish Date: *4/9*

Notes: *FASTENING OF PLASTERBOARD REQUIRES INSPECTION BEFORE APPLYING MUD*
DUMPSTER MUST BE PICKED UP NO LATER THAN 30 DAYS AFTER DELIVERY

Exhibit 7: Sample of Calendar Schedule

| Project   *SMITH JOB* | | | Start Date: *3/1* | |
| Address: *321 W. 6TH* | | | Finish Date: *4/9* | |
Monday	Tuesday	Wednesday	Thursday	Friday
1 *SITE PREP & LAYOUT*	**2** *EXCAVATION*	**3** *FORM WORK* ⊢────────	**4** ────┘ ✓	**5** *POUR CONCRETE*
8 *REMOVE FORMS*	**9** *UNDER FLOOR WORK & POSTS & BEAMS*	**10** *INSULATION* ✓ *DRAINPIPES* ✓ *BACKFILL*	**11** *DECKING* *WALL FRAMING* ⊢────	**12** ──── *CLEAN-UP*
WALLS ⊢┐ **15** ⊢──────┘	**16** *ROOF FRAMING*	**17** *SHEATHING*	**18** *ROOFING*	*DOORS & WINDOWS* **19** ──────────┘
22 *GUTTERS ROUGH ELECT*	✓ ✓ **23** *INSPECTIONS INSULATION* ✓ *(WALLS & ATTIC)*	**24** *BUILDING DRY-OUT SIDING*	✓ **25** *(PLASTER BOARD)* *PLASTER WORK* ⊢──── *EXT. TRIM*	**26** ────
29 *PLASTER* ⊢──	*INTERIOR* **30** *PAINT (UNDER COAT)* *EXTERIOR PAINT* ────────	**31** *FINISH* ────	*CARPENTRY* **1** ────┘	**2** *CLEAN-UP FINISH GRADING*
5 *INT. PAINTING & STAINING* ⊢──── *LANDSCAPING* ⊢────	**6** ──── ────	**7** *FINISH ELECT* *CARPETING*	*MISC.* ⑧ *CLEAN-UP*	**9** *FINAL INSPECTION* ✓

Notes:
① *PRIOR TO START, WORK OUT VARIOUS DETAILS W/OWNER & ORDER CRITICAL ITEMS*
✓ *INDICATES INSPECTION REQUIRED*
⑧ *OPTIONAL DATE FOR FINAL INSPECTION*

Quick Reference Tool

Activity

Any work on a construction project that has a specific beginning and end. A task or job that has to be done within the project. When used in the context of CPM scheduling, no new activity can start until its originating event is completed; each activity must be completed before the event to which it leads can begin (see Rule of Dependency.)

Activity Duration

See Duration.

Bar Chart Scheduling

A quick and easy method of scheduling that details the relationships between various work activities. A bar chart is used to create a graph of a construction project showing those overlapping activities and at what point in the project, in terms of workdays, each activity is expected to begin and end.

Branching-Out

Pertains to Critical Path Method of scheduling. Branching out occurs when construction activities that are not dependent upon one another can start at the same timepoint within a CPM schedule. That point is where the diagram will branch out.

Calendar Scheduling

As used in this manual, calendar scheduling is basically placing a bar chart on a calendar. This form of scheduling is practical for small construction projects. However, all projects can benefit from calendar scheduling because it pinpoints construction activities to specific dates.

Calendar scheduling has the advantage of taking into account weekends, holidays, and vacations.

Checklist

A list of all the phases (work activities) of which the project is composed. It is the "break-down" of a project into its parts.

This break-down list becomes a checklist when it is used to make certain that all parts of the project have been included in the project's schedule. (See Project Breakdown and Duration Checklist.)

CPM Total Time

The sum of the durations of all activities lying along the critical path of a CPM diagram represents the total time duration (in terms of workdays) for the project.

It is the least amount of time in which the project can be completed (assuming estimated duration times for each activity prove to be accurate).

Critical Path Method (CPM)

This method of scheduling shows a construction project in diagram form. It shows the longest path (in terms of adding up how long each part of the project takes along the different routes of the diagram) through a project and the effect delays have on the rest of the project.

Every project has a series of critical tasks that determine the minimum time needed to complete the entire project. When two or more activities are scheduled simultaneously, one "path" may take longer than the others; that is the critical path.

Critical Activities

Critical activities are tasks in a critical path diagram that have no float time (see Float Time). These activities lie on the critical path for a project. A delay in any one of these activities will cause a delay for the rest of the project.

Non-critical activities have float time (spare time) in which to be completed.

Critical Items

Materials, supplies and/or services for a construction project that need to be ordered or planned well in advance of actual construction or installation.

Daily Reports

A formal, written method of tracking progress. Each subcontractor and your foreman or supervisor should submit a daily report showing what work was actually accomplished during the day and what work is planned for the next day.

The information obtained from daily reports will be compared to the project's schedule to determine if the project is on, ahead, or behind schedule.

Daily Schedule

That part of a daily report (see Daily Report) that describes the work to be done the following workday.

Direct Costs

Those costs directly related to a construction project. This would include any labor (including your own) and materials needed to complete the project. Direct costs do not include "overhead" expenses (see Indirect Costs).

Dummy Lines (Dummies)

Dotted lines, in CPM diagraming, that connect certain events (see Events) within a construction project. Dummy lines (dotted lines) are used instead of solid lines when one or both of the following situations need to be indicated:

- There is no time-lag between the connected events.
- For identification purposes, it is necessary to create an artificial event to give one work activity a different event number than another activity.

Duration

An estimated length of time to complete a phase or activity of a construction project. For example, the duration of excavation for a certain project could be two (2) days.

The duration of any work activity is dependent upon such factors as the number and skill of workers performing the activity and other conditions that could affect how long the activity will take.

On a CPM diagram, the duration time (in terms of workdays) is placed under the corresponding activity.

Earliest Event Time

In CPM scheduling an event represents the end of one construction activity and the beginning of another. In terms of work days, the earliest event time is the earliest point that each event can take place within a project.

On a CPM diagram the earliest event number of workdays is typically placed in a rectangular box next to the event number.

Estimate

In the context of scheduling, an estimate is a calculated guess regarding the length of time it will take to complete each of the activities of a construction project.

Estimating this duration time for project activities is best accomplished when based on previously recorded information from earlier construction projects.

Evaluation

An organized (written) process for comparing estimated time (activity duration) with the actual time an activity took to complete. Evaluation procedures are essential for establishing accurate estimating for future projects.

Event

A term used in CPM scheduling to denote the end of one activity in a project and the beginning of another.

Float Time

Extra time available to complete each task without delaying final completion of the entire project. Some portions of the work have zero float time, such as those activities which are "critical" (see Critical Activities).

Identifying which construction activities have time to spare and which do not will enable the contractor to make adjustments in the scheduling of the project.

Indirect Costs

These are your "overhead" expenses. These expenses stem from the cost of doing business. Indirect costs would include such items as vehicle expenses, office expenses, insurance, etc.

Inspections

Various parts of a construction project will require an official inspection by an agent(s) of the local (in relation to the construction project) building department. Until such an inspection is made, no further work may be performed that would cover the work to be inspected.

Project scheduling should identify where and when inspections are required and allot the necessary time to perform these inspections.

In some instances, the contract may stipulate other inspections by architects, engineers, and/or loan officers. Such inspections will also need to be scheduled.

Just-in-time Deliveries

Having deliveries of materials and supplies delivered as you need them, although you may have purchased them in advance. Using this method reduces:

- Clutter around the project site
- Material shuffling
- The chance of injury or theft

Latest Event Time

The latest event time represents the maximum number of workdays into the project in which a particular phase (event) needs to be completed in order not to delay the overall project.

"Laws" of Construction Nature

There are two "laws" of construction nature for the contractor to take into account when scheduling:

- The job will always take longer.
- The job will always cost more.

It is sometimes said that these "laws" run in a "3x2" manner: The job will take three times as long and cost twice as much, or vice versa.

A contractor can best deal with these "laws" by establishing organized (written) methods of estimating, scheduling, and evaluating projects.

Murphy's Law

Anything that can go wrong, will. An experienced contractor will factor-in "Murphy's Law" when developing a project schedule.

Personalized Scheduling

A contractor can develop a method for scheduling projects that uses aspects from more than one scheduling system. A personalized system may be a combination of a calendar, bar chart, and/or critical path method of scheduling.

A contractor will develop the best personalized system by first learning the basics of scheduling systems, then using these systems on actual projects to determine what works best for their specialty.

Preliminary Schedule

Using your estimate sheet and other project documents, such as the contract, plans, and other specifications, a preliminary schedule is developed as an agenda for the pre-project meeting. This schedule is a starting place for coordinating the activities of all the major parties (owners, architects, engineers, subcontractors, etc.) associated with the project and is used to determine where potential conflicts could arise.

Pre-project Meeting

A time and place where all the major parties (owners, architects, engineers, subcontractors, etc.) associated with the project get together and discuss the flow of activities for the project. The purpose of the meeting is to establish a mutual understanding of the scope and timing of the project and to identify and discuss potential problems.

Progress Report

A progress report is basically a written "what got done" list. This list can be written on a daily, weekly and/or monthly basis depending upon the size of the project.

The information on the progress report is compared to the actual schedule to evaluate if the project is on, ahead, or behind the estimated schedule.

Project Breakdown and Duration Checklist

A project "breakdown" is a list of the parts of a construction project such as excavation, form work, setting posts and beams, etc. This written list is developed to check and make certain that all parts of the project are included within the schedule.

For scheduling purposes, the parts of the project will be listed in the order in which they can be performed. Before listing any work activity, the contractor will make certain that any other activity that needs to be completed first has already been listed. (See Rule of Dependency.)

For each activity listed, an estimate of the time needed to complete that activity is written down. This is the duration of that activity.

Realistic schedule

A realistic schedule is one that is both workable and sequential.

Rule of Dependency

The rule of dependency states that all work activity for a project is listed or diagramed in the proper sequence. This sequence is based upon asking: "What must first be completed before this part of the project can begin." (See Sequential Schedule.)

Sequential Schedule

A sequential schedule is one that has all the activities in proper sequence based upon the rule of dependency. For example, rafter installation could not be scheduled before the walls are put up.

Workable Schedule

A workable schedule is one that takes into consideration the ability of the workers to accomplish a part of a construction project. For example, scheduling the work of three carpenters when you only have two is not a workable schedule. (See Realistic Schedule.)

You, Our Customer

As our customer, we are happy to demonstrate our customer service to you. As with all our courses, we at the Academy offer our services to you through these courses. If you have questions or problems, we would be happy to talk to you.

We ask that you follow this process:

1. Read the course and check out the Bibliography for more leads on your question. If you have a library available, you can check out the books or ask the librarian how to find them. Please check at least one resource before contacting us.

2. Frame your question(s) on paper before contacting us. You will find it very useful to write your question down. In this way you make sure you know exactly what you want to ask.

3. Our first response to your question will usually be to refer you to other courses in the Advantage Contractor Business Success Series, or Resources in the courses. We want you to learn how to find information on your own. Developing skill at finding information gives you a powerful advantage as a contractor. If you rely on us for your information, you are limited and become dependent on us. Remember, you are an **independent** construction contractor.

4. If, after looking for information on your own, you still have a question, please contact us. We assume at this point that your question will now be more detailed, having gathered some information. However, we may still refer you to a specific source which will answer your question. The object of this process will be similar to what a teacher would do in assisting you to learn how to ask informed questions and find new sources of answers.

How to contact us in order of our preference:

A. E-Mail: question@acbss.com
B. Fax inquiry: 541-344-5387
C. US Mail: 83 Centennial Loop, Eugene, OR 97401
D. Phone: 541-344-1442

Thanks for your cooperation in following this process.

State Offices that Provide Small Business Help

Alabama
Alabama Development Office
State Capitol
Montgomery, AL 36130
(800) 248-0333* (205) 263-0048

Alaska
Division of Economic Development
Department of Commerce and Economic
    Development
PO Box D
Juneau, AK 99811
(907) 465-2017

Arizona
Office of Business Finance
Department of Commerce
3800 North Central Avenue
Suite 1500
Phoenix, AZ 85012
(602) 280-1341

Arkansas
Small Business Information Center
Industrial Development Commission
State Capitol Mall
Room 4C-300
Little Rock, AR 72201
(501) 682-5275

California
Office of Small Business
Department of Commerce
801 K Street, Suite 1700
Sacramento, CA 95814
(916) 327-4357 (916) 445-6545

Colorado
One-Stop Assistance Center
1560 Broadway, Suite 1530
Denver, CO 80202
(800) 333-7798 (303) 592-5920

Connecticut
Small Business Services
Department of Economic Development
865 Brook Street
Rocky Hill, CN 06067
(203) 258-4269

Delaware
Development Office
PO Box 1401
99 Kings Highway
Dover, DE 19903
(302) 736-4271

District of Columbia
Office of Business and Economic
    Development
Tenth Floor
717 14th Street NW
Washington, DC 20005
(202) 727-6600

Florida
Bureau of Business Assistance
Department of Commerce
107 West Gaines Street, Room 443
Tallahassee, FL 32399-2000
(800) 342-0771*

* In state calling only

Georgia
Department of Community Affairs
100 Peachtree Street, Suite 1200
Atlanta, GA 30303
(404) 656-6200

Hawaii
Small Business Information Service
737 Bishop Street, Suite 1900
Honolulu, HI 96813
(808) 578-7645 (808) 543-6691

Idaho
Economic Development Division
Department of Commerce
700 State Street
Boise, ID 83720-2700
(208) 334-2470

Illinois
Small Business Assistance Bureau
Department of Commerce and
    Community Affairs
620 East Adams Street
Springfield, IL 62701
(800) 252-2923*

Indiana
Ombudsman's Office
Business Development Division
Department of Commerce
One North Capitol, Suite 700
Indianapolis, IN 46204-2288
(800) 824-2476* (317) 232-7304

Iowa
Bureau of Small Business Development
Department of Economic Development
200 East Grand Avenue
Des Moines, IA 50309
(800) 532-1216* (515) 242-4899

Kansas
Division of Existing Industry
Development
400 SW Eighth Street
Topeka, KS 66603
(785) 296-5298

Kentucky
Division of Small Business
Capitol Plaza Tower
Frankfort, KY 40601
(800) 626-2250* (502) 564-4252

Louisiana
Development Division
Office of Commerce and Industry
PO Box 94185
Baton Rouge, LA 70804-9185
(504) 342-5365

Maine
Business Development Division
State Development Office
State House
Augusta, ME 04333
(800) 872-3838* (207) 289-3153

Maryland
Division of Business Development
Department of Economic and
Employment Development
217 East Redwood Street
Baltimore, MD 21202
(800) 873-7232 (301) 333-6996

Massachusetts
Office of Business Development
100 Cambridge Street
13th Floor
Boston, MA 02202
(617) 727-3206

* In state calling only

Michigan

Michigan Business Ombudsman
Department of Commerce
PO Box 30107
Lansing, MI 48909
(800) 232-2727* (517) 373-6241

Minnesota

Small Business Assistance Office
Department of Trade and Economic
Development
900 American Center Building
150 East Kellogg Boulevard
St. Paul, MN 55101
(800) 652-9747 (612) 296-3871

Mississippi

Small Business Bureau
Research and Development Center
PO Box 849
Jackson, MS 39205
(601) 359-3552

Missouri

Small Business Bureau
Research and Development Center
PO Box 118
Jefferson City, MO 65102
(314) 751-4982 (314) 751-8411

Montana

Business Assistance Division
Department of Commerce
1424 Ninth Ave.
Helena, MT 59620
(800) 221-8015* (406) 444-2801

Nebraska

Existing Business Division
Department of Economic Development
PO Box 94666
301 Centennial Mall South
Lincoln, NE 68509-4666
(402) 471-3782

Nevada

Nevada Commission of Economic
Development
Capitol Complex
Carson City, NV 89710
(702) 687-4325

New Hampshire

Small Business Development Center
University Center
400 Commercial Street, Room 311
Manchester, NH 03101
(603) 625-4522

New Jersey

Office of Small Business Assistance
Department of Commerce and Economic
Development
20 West State Street, CN 835
Trenton, NJ 08625
(609) 984-4442

New Mexico

Economic Development Division
Department of Economic Development
1100 St. Francis Drive
Santa Fe, NM 87503
(505) 827-0300

New York

Division for Small Business
Department of Economic Development
1515 Broadway
51st Floor
New York, NY 10036
(212) 827-6150

North Carolina

Small Business Development Division
Department of Economic and
Community Development
Dobbs Building, Room 2019
430 North Salisbury Street
Raleigh, NC 27611
(919) 733-2810

* In state calling only

North Dakota

Small Business Coordinator
Economic Development Commission
Liberty Memorial Building
604 East Boulevard
Bismark, ND 58505
(701) 224-2810

Ohio

Small and Developing Business Division
Department of Development
PO Box 1001
Columbus, OH 43266-0101
(800) 248-4040* (614) 466-4232

Oklahoma

Oklahoma Department of Commerce
PO Box 26980
6601 N. Broadway Extension
Oklahoma City, OK 73126-0980
(800) 477-6552* (405) 843-9770

Oregon

Economic Development Department
775 Summer Street NE
Salem, OR 97310
(800) 233-3306* (503) 373-1200

Pennsylvania

Bureau of Small Business and
   Appalachian Development
Department of Commerce
461 Forum Building
Harrisburg, PA 17120
(717) 783-5700

Puerto Rico

Commonwealth Department of
   Commerce
Box S
4275 Old San Juan Station
San Juan, PR 00905
(809) 721-3290

Rhode Island

Business Development Division
Department of Economic Development
Seven Jackson Walkway
Providence, RI 02903
(401) 277-2601

South Carolina

Enterprise Development
PO Box 1149
Columbia, SC 29202
(800) 922-6684* (803) 737-0888

South Dakota

Governor's Office of Economic
   Development
Capital Lake Plaza
711 Wells Avenue
Pierre, SD 57501
(800) 872-6190* (605) 773-5032

Tennessee

Small Business Office
Department of Economic and
Community Development
320 Sixth Avenue North
Seventh Floor
Rachel Jackson Building
Nashville, TN 37219
(800) 872-7201* (615) 741-2626

Texas

Small Building Division
Department of Commerce
Economic Development Commission
PO Box 12728
Capitol Station
410 East Fifth Street
Austin, TX 78711
(800) 888-0511 (512) 472-5059

* In state calling only

Utah
Small Business Development Center
102 West 500 South, Suite 315
Salt Lake City, UT 84101
(801) 581-7905

Vermont
Agency of Development and Community
    Affairs
The Pavilion
109 State Street
Montpelier, VT 05609
(800) 622-4553* (802) 828-3221

Virginia
Small Business and Financial Services
Department of Economic Development
PO Box 798
1000 Washington Building
Richmond, VA 23206
(804) 371-8252

Washington
Small Business Development Center
245 Todd Hall
Washington State University
Pullman, WA 99164-4727
(509) 335-1576

West Virginia
Small Business Development Center
    Division
1115 Virginia Street East
Charleston, WV 25301
(304) 348-2960

Wisconsin
Public Information Bureau
Department of Development
PO Box 7970
123 West Washington Avenue
Madison, WI 53707
(800) 435-7287* (608) 266-1018

Wyoming
Economic Development and
Stabilization Board
Herschler Building
Cheyenne, WY 82002
(307) 777-7287

* In state calling only
Source: National Association for the Self-
Employed,
USA TODAY research

Resources

The following sources are generally recognized as associated members of the building industry that have impact on standards and guidelines of business operations. You can contact these sources to get specific information on products and business ideas in your specific trade or business area. In some cases you can go to a local chapter for help. These associations will be promoting their product or service, but will also be able to answer many business, technical and product questions.

Air Conditioning Contractors of America (ACCA)
1513 16th St. NW
Washington, DC 20036

Air Conditioning and Refrigeration Institute
4301 N. Fairfax Dr. Suite 425
Arlington, VA 22203
(703) 524-8800

Aluminum Association (AA)
900 19th St. NW, Ste. 300
Washington, DC 20006
(202) 862-5100

American Association of Nurserymen
1250 I St. NW, Suite 500
Washington, DC 20005
(202) 789-2900

American Building Contractors Assn.
PO Box 2772
Cypress, CA 90630
(714) 828-4760
http://www.netcom.com/~w-e/abca.html

American Concrete Institute (ACI)
P.O. Box 19150
Detroit, MI 48219

American Gas Association
1515 Wilson Blvd.
Arlington, VA 22209
(703) 841-8589

American Hardboard Association
520 N. Hicks Rd.
Palatine, IL 60067
(312) 934-8800

American Hardware Manufacturers Association (AHMA)
801 N. Plaza Drive
Schaumburg, IL 60173-4977
(847) 605-1025

American Institute of Building Design
991 Post Rd. E.
Westport, CT 06880
(800) 366-2423

American Institute of Steel Construction, Inc.
1 E. Wacker Dr., Ste. 3100
Chicago, IL 60601-2001
(312) 670-2400

American Institute of Timber Construction (AITC)
11818 SE Mill Plain Blvd., Ste. 415
Vancouver, WA 98684
(206) 254-9132

**American Insurance
Association (AIA)**
>1130 Connecticut Ave. NW, Ste. 1000
>Washington, DC 20036
>(202) 828-7100

**American Iron and Steel Institute
(AISI)**
>1133 15th St. NW
>Washington, DC 20005
>(202) 452-7100

America Lighting Association
>World Trade Center
>PO Box 420288
>Dallas, TX 75342-0288
>(800) 605-4448

**American National Standards
Institute (ANSI)**
>11 W. 42nd St., 13th floor
>New York, NY 10036
>(212) 642-4900

American Plywood Association (APA)
>P.O. Box 11700
>Tacoma, WA 98411
>(206) 565-6600

**American Society of Heating,
Refrigeration and Air Conditioning
Engineers**
>1791 Tullie Circle NE
>Atlanta, GA 30329
>(404) 636-8400

American Society of Home Inspectors
>85 W. Algonquin Rd., Suite 360
>Arlington Heights, IL 60005
>(800) 743-ASHI (2744)

American Society of Interior Designers
>608 Massachusetts Ave. NW
>Washington, DC 20002-6006
>(202) 546-3480

**American Society of Testing Materials
(ASTM)**
>100 Bar Harbor Dr.
>West Conshohocken, PA 19428-2959
>(610) 832-9500

American Solar Energy Society (ASES)
>2400 Central Ave. Suite G1
>Boulder, CO 80301
>(303) 443-3130

American Subcontractors Association
>1004 Duke St.
>Alexandria, VA 22314
>(703) 684-3450
>ASAoffice@aol.com

American Welding Society, Inc. (AWS)
>550 LeJeune Rd. NW, P.O. Box 351040
>Miami, FL 33135
>(305) 443-9353

**American Wood-Preservers
Association (AWPA)**
>P.O. Box 286
>Woodstock, MD 21163-0286
>(410) 465-3169

**American Wood Preservers Bureau
(AWPB)**
>P.O. Box 5283
>Springfield, VA 22150
>(703)339-6660

**American Wood Preservers Institute
(AWPI)**
>1945 Old Gallows Rd., Ste. 550
>Vienna, VA 22182

Appraisal Institute
>875 N. Michigan Ave. Suite 2400
>Chicago, IL 60611-1980
>(312) 335-4100

Architectural Woodwork Institute
13924 Braddock Rd. Suite 100
Centreville, VA 22020-1910
(703) 222-1100

Asphalt Roofing Manufacturers
6288 Montrose Rd.
Rockville, MD 20852
(301) 231-9050

Association for Preservation Technology
PO Box 3511
Williamsburgh, VA 23187
(703) 373-1621

Association for Safe & Accessible Products
1511 K. St., N. W., Suite 600
Washington, OR 20005-4905
(202) 347-8200
asapdc@aol.com

Association of Construction Inspectors
8383 E. Evans St.
Scottsdale, AZ 85260
(602) 998-8021
aci@iami.org
http://iami.org/aci.html

Association of Home Appliance Manufacturers
20 N. Wacker Dr.
Chicago, IL 60606-2806
(312) 984-5800

Brick Institute of America (BIA)
11490 Commerce Park Dr.
Reston, VA 22091
(703) 620-0010

Building Systems Councils of NAHB
15th & M Streets NW
Washington, DC 20005

Canadian Home Builders' Association
150 Laurier Ave. W. Suite 200
Ottawa, ON K1P 5J4 Canada
(613) 230-3060

Canadian Retail Hardware Association (CRHA)
6800 Campobello Rd.
Mississauga, ON L5N 2L8 Canada
(905) 821-3470

The Carpet and Rug Institute
PO Box 2049
Dalton, GA 30722-2048
(706) 278-3176

Cast Iron Soil Pipe Institute
5939 Shallowford Rd. Suite 419
Chattanooga, TN 37421
615-892-0137

Cedar Shake and Shingle Bureau
515 116th Ave. NW, Ste. 275
Bellevue, WA 98004-5294
(206) 453-1323

Cellulose Insulation Manufacturers Association
136 S. Keowee St.
Dayton, OH 45402
(513) 222-2464
assocoffice@delphi.com
ah803@dayton.wright.edu

Ceramic Tile Institute of America
800 Roosevelt Rd. Bldg C, Suite 20
Glen Ellyn, IL 60137
(708) 545-9415

Concrete Reinforcing Steel Institute (CRSI)
933 Plum Grove Rd.
Schaumburg, IL 60173

Decorative Laminate Products Association
13924 Braddock Rd., Suite 100
Centreville, VA 22020
(800) 684-3572

Energy Efficiency and Renewable Energy Clearinghouse (EREC)
PO Box 3048
Merrifield, VA 22116
(800) 363-3732
doe.erec@nciinc.com
http://www.erecbbs.nciinc.com

The Environmental Information Assn.
4915 Auburn Ave., Suite 303
Bethesda, MD 20814
(301) 961-4999

Forest Products Research Society
2801 Marshall Court
Madison, WI 53705
(608) 231-1361

Garage Door Hardware Association
2850 S. Ocean Blvd., Suite 311
Palm Beach, FL 33480-5535
(407) 533-0991

Gypsum Association (GA)
810 1st St. NE, Suite 510
Washington, DC 20002
(202) 289-5440

Hardwood Plywood Manufacturer's Association (HPMA)
1825 Michael Faraday Dr., P.O. Box 2789
Reston, VA 22090

Home Automation Association
808 17th St. NW, Suite 200
Washington, DC 20006-3910
(202) 223-9669
75250.1274@copuserve.com

Home Fashion Products Association
355 Lexington Ave. 17th Fl.
New York, NY 10017-6603

Home Improvement Research Institute
400 Knightsbridge Pkwy
Lincolnshire, IL 60069-3646
847-634-4368

Home Inspection Institute of America
314 Main St.
PO Box 4174
Yalesville Wallingford, CT 06492
(203) 284-2311
homeinspi@aol.com

Home Ventilating Institute
30 W. University Dr.
Arlington Heights, IL 60004-1806
(708) 394-0150

International Masonry Institute
823 15th St. NW
Washington, DC 20005
(202) 783-3908

International Wood Products Assn.
4214 Kings St. W.
Alexandria, VA 22302
(703) 820-6696
info@ihpa.org
http//www.ihpa.org

Italian Tile Association
305 Madison Ave., Suite 3120
New York, NY 10165-0111
(212) 661-0435

Kitchen Cabinet Manufacturers Association
1899 Preston White Dr.
Reston, VA 22091
(703) 264-1690

Manufactured Housing Institute
1745 Jefferson Davis Hwy., Ste. 511
Arlington, VA 22202

Maple Flooring Manufacturers Association
60 Revere Dr., Suite 500
Northbrook, IL 60062
(708) 480-9138

Mechanical Contractors Association of America
1385 Piccard Dr.
Rockville, MD 20850
(301) 869-5800

Metal Building Manufacturers Association (MBMA)
2130 Keith Building
Cleveland, OH 44115

Metal Lath/Steel Framing Association Division
600 5. Federal St., Ste. 400
Chicago, IL 60605
(312) 922-6222

Mineral Insulation Manufacturers Association
1420 King St.
Alexandria, VA 22314

National Assn. of Brick Distributors
1600 Spring Hill Rd., Suite 305
Vienna, VA 22182
(703) 749-6223

National Association of Electrical Distributors
45 Danbury Rd.
Wilton, CT 06897
(203) 834-1908

National Association of Home Builders (NAHB)
1201 15th St., NW
Washington, DC 20005-2800
(202) 822-0200

National Association of Home Builders Remodelers Council
1201 15th St., N. W.
Washington, DC 20005-2800
(800) 368-5242 Ext. 216

National Association of Home Inspectors
4248 Park Glen Rd.
Minneapolis, MN 55416
(800) 448-3942
assnhdqs@usinternet.com

National Association of Plumbing-Heating-Cooling Contractors
PO Box 6808
Falls Church, VA 22040
(800) 533-7694
naphcc@naphcc.org
http://www.naphcc.org

National Association of Real Estate Appraisers
8383 E. Evans Rd.
Scottsdale, AZ 85260
(602) 948-8000

National Association of the Remodeling Industry (NARI)
4900 Seminary Rd., Suite 320
Alexandria, VA 22311
(800) 966-7601

National Association of Women in Construction
327 S. Adams St.
Fort Worth, TX 76104-1002
(800) 552-3506

National Concrete Masonry Association (NCMA)
2302 Horse Pen Rd.
Herndon, VA 22071-3499
(703) 713-1900

National Decorating Products Association (NDPA)
1050 N. Lindbergh Blvd.
St. Louis, MO 63132-2994
(314) 991-3470

National Fire Protection Association (NFPA)
1 Batterymarch Park, P.O. Box 9101
Quincy, MA 02269-9101
(617) 770-3000

National Fire Sprinkler Association
Robin Hill Corp. Pk., Rt. 22, Box 1
Patterson, NY 12563
(617) 770-3000

National Forest Products Association
1250 Connecticut Ave. NW, Ste. 200
Washington, DC 20036
(202) 463-2700

National Kitchen and Bath Association (NKBA)
687 Willow Grove St.
Hackettstown, NJ 07840
(908) 852-0033

National Lime Association (MA)
3601 N. Fairfax Dr.
Arlington, VA 22201
(703) 243-5463

National Oak Flooring Manufacturers Association
PO Box 3009
Memphis, TN 38173
(901) 526-5016

National Particleboard Association (NPA)
18928 Premiere Ct.
Gaithersburg, MD 20879-1569
(301) 670-0604

National Pest Control Association (NPCA)
8100 Oak St.
Dunn Loring, VA 22027
(703) 573-8330

National Retail Hardware Assn.
5822 W. 74th St.
Indianapolis, IN 46278-1787
(317) 290-0338

National Roofing Contractors Association
10255 W. Higgins Rd., Suite 600
Rosemont, IL 60018
(800) 323-9545

National Spa and Pool Institute
2111 Eisenhower Ave.
Alexandria, VA 22314-4698
(703) 838-0083
http://www.resourcecenter.com

National Terrazzo and Mosaic Assn.
3166 Des Plaines Ave., Suite 121
Des Plaines, IL 60018-4223
(800) 323-9736

National Wood Flooring Assn.
233 Old Meremac Station Rd.
Manchester, MO 63021
(314)391-5161

National Wood Window and Door Assn.
1400 E. Touhy Ave., Suite 470
Des Plaines, IL 60018-3305
(800) 233-2301
nwwda@ais.net
http://www.nwwda.org

Noise Control Association
680 Rainier Ln.
Port Ludlow, WA 98365
(360) 437-0814

Northern American Insulation Manufacturers
44 Canal Center Plaza, Suite 310
Alexandria, VA 22314
(703) 684-0084

Oak Flooring Institute/National Oak Flooring Manufacturers Association
PO Box 3009
Memphis, TN 38173-0009
(901) 526-5016

Painting and Decorating Contractors of America (PDCA)
3913 Old Lee Hwy. #33-B
Fairfax, VA 22030
(800) 332-PDCA.

Portland Cement Association (PCA)
5420 Old Orchard Road
Skokie, IL 60077
(708) 966-6200

Resilient Floor Covering Institute
966 Hungerford Dr., Suite 12-B
Rockville, MD 20850-1714
(301) 340-8580

Roofing Industry Education Institute
14 Inverness Dr., Suite H-110
Englewood, CO 80112-5625
(303) 790-7200

Safe Building Alliance
655 15th St., N. W., Suite 1200
Washington, DC 20005-5701
(202) 879-5120

Sealed Insulating Glass Manufacturers Association
401 N. Michigan Ave.
Chicago, IL 60611-4212
(312) 644-6610
sigma@sba.com

Sheet Metal and Air Conditioning Contractor's National Association
P.O. Box 70
Merrifield, VA 22116
703-790-9890

Society of Certified Kitchen Designers
687 Willow Grove St.
Hackettstown, NJ 07840
(800) 843-6522

Society of the Plastics Industry (SPI) Spray Polyurethane Foam Division
1801 K. St., N. W., Suite 600K
Washington, DC 20006-1031
(800) 523-6154

Solar Energy Industries Association
122 C St., N. W., Fourth Floor
Washington, DC 20001
(202) 383-2600

Solar Rating and Certification Corp.
122 C St., N. W., Fourth Floor
Washington, DC 20001
(202) 383-2650

Southern Forest Products Association (SFPA)
P.O. Box 641770
Kenner, LA 70064-1700
(504) 443-4464
http://www.southernpine.com

Southern Pine Council
PO Box 641770
Kenner, LA 70064-1700
(504) 443-4464
http://www.southernpine.com

Southwest Research & Information Center (SRI)
P.O. Box 4524
Albuquerque, NM 87106
505-262-1862

Steel Joist Institute (SJI)
1205 48th Ave. N., Ste. A
Myrtle Beach, SC 29577

Steel Window Institute (SWI)
c/o Thomas Assocs., Inc.
2130 Keith Building
Cleveland, OH 44115

Tile Contractors Assn. of America
11501 Georgia Ave., Suite 203
Wheaton, MD 20902
(800) OKK-TILE (655-8458)

Tile Council of America (TCA)
P.O. Box 1787
Clemson, SC 29633-1787
(864) 646-TILE (8453)

Truss Plate Institute (TPI)
583 D'Onofrio Dr., Ste. 200
Madison, WI 53719
608-833-5900

Underwriters' Laboratories (UL)
333 Pfingsten Road
Northbrook, IL 60062

United American Contractors Assn.
85 Central St.
Boston, MA 02109
(617) 357-4470

Vinyl Siding Institute Div. of the Society of the Plastics Industry
1275 K. St., N. W., Suite 400
Washington, DC 20005
(202) 371-5200

Vinyl Window & Door Institute Div. of the Society of the Plastics Industry
1275 K. St., N. W., Suite 400
Washington, DC 20005
(202) 371-5200

Western Red Cedar Lumber Association
1100-555 Burrard St.
Vancouver, BC V7x 1S7
Canada
(604) 684-0266
wrcla@cofiho.cofi.org
http://www.cofi.org/WRCLA

Western Wood Products Association (WWPA)
Yeon Building, 522 SW 5th Ave., Suite 400
Portland, OR 97204-2122
503-224-3930

Women Construction Owners & Executives, USA
4849 Connecticut Ave., N. W., Suite 706
Washington, DC 20008-5838
(800) 788-3548
wcoeusa@aol.com

Bibliography

Bar Chart Scheduling for Residential Construction
Love, Craftsman

CPM Construction Scheduler's Manual
Hutchins, McGraw-Hill

Critical Path Methods in Construction
Avtill, Wiley

Managing Projects with Microsoft
Lowery, Wiley

Means Project Planning and Contracting
Pierce, Means

Means Scheduling Manual
Horsley, Means

Project Planning, Scheduling and Control in Construction
Popescu, Wiley

Project Scheduler Software
Scitor

Web Sites

These web site addresses have information about the topics covered in this course. You will have to look around the site for the information you need. You can benefit from using e-mail to contact people at the site about your questions. In addition, there are usually links to other sites that may be of interest.

If you are a veteran in using the internet, you already know that searching the internet can be frustrating and time consuming. Set out your questions on paper before you go to the internet. Then attempt to stick with these issues in your searching. Refrain from taking side trips until you have your questions answered.

Be sure to check our web site at:

http://www.acbss.com

Canadian Home Builders Association
http://www.buildermanual.com

http://www.magi.com/~homes/

Entreprenuer Magazine
http://www.entrepreurmag.com

Journal of Light Construction Builder's Forum
http://www.bginet.com/jlcforum/index.html

National Association of the Remodeling Industry
http://www.nari.org

National Association of Women in Construction
http://www.nawic@onramp.net (e-mail address)

Northwest Build Net
http://www.nwbuildnet.com

Women Construction Owners and Executives
http://www.wcoeusa@aol.com (e-mail address)

http://www.abuildnet.com

http://www.acns.nwu.edu/library/virtual/v_cone.html

http://www.aecinfo.com/construc/companies/const_man.html

http://www.build.com

http://www.builderbooksite.com

http://www.BuildingOnLine.com

http://www.BuildingTechBooks.com

http://www.b.w.co.uk/BIW/sainsbury/js-time3.htm

http://www.construction-institute.org/programs/97cpi.htm

http://www.edgeonline.com

http://www.isquare.com

http://www.mcgraw-hill.inforonics.com/mghp/mgh/
710021003browse.shtml

http://www.missouri.edu/~pdc/

http://www.neosoft.com/~benchmrx/rcps.ascii

http://www.smartbiz.com

Remodeling Related

http://www.longrun.onweb.com/remodellinks.html

http://www.probuilder.com/home/home.html

http://www.builderweb .com

Web sites are constantly changing. These sites may change or even disappear. Those sites that are operated by contracting organizations are likely to be the most stable. Your search could lead to other new sites. Let us know if you find a good one.

Index